# Into a New Country

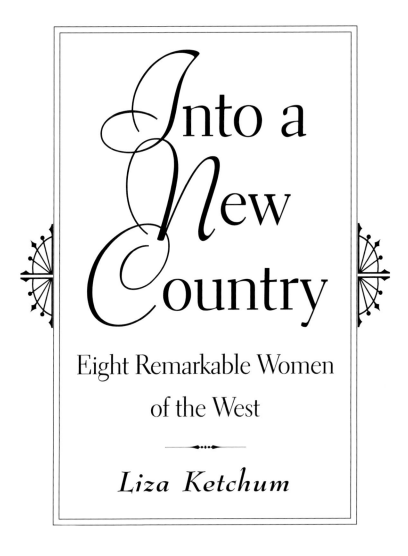

# Into a New Country

## Eight Remarkable Women of the West

### Liza Ketchum

LITTLE, BROWN AND COMPANY

BOSTON  NEW YORK  LONDON

Also by Liza Ketchum:
*The Gold Rush*

First Edition

Design: Lisa Diercks
Map illustration: Ethan K. Murrow

Library of Congress Cataloging-in-Publication Data
Ketchum, Liza.
Into a New Country : eight remarkable women of the West / by Liza Ketchum—1st ed.
   p.  cm.
   Summary: Presents the history of the West through eight biographies of women,
including Susan Magoffin, Lotta Crabtree, and Biddy Mason.
   ISBN 0-316-49597-2 (hc)
   1. Women pioneers—West (U.S.)—Biography—Juvenile literature. 2. West (U.S.)—
Biography—Juvenile literature. 3. Frontier and pioneer life—West (U.S.)—Juvenile
literature. [1. Pioneers. 2. Women—Biography. 3. West (U.S.)—Biography. 4. Frontier
and pioneer life—West (U.S.)] I. Title.
F596.K45 2000
978'.0082—dc21

99-052358

10 9 8 7 6 5 4 3 2 1

MV

Printed in the United States of America

*In memory of my friend*

*Anne Turid Sato,*

*a twentieth-century pioneer*

# Contents

# Into a New Country

I MAGINE A CREEK THAT begins as a trickle in the mountains, fills its banks in a sudden rainstorm, then roars downstream in a flash flood, sweeping away everything in its path. This was what happened in the American West in the nineteenth century. Beginning in the 1820s, a trickle of pioneers began to explore the frontier beyond the Mississippi River. By the 1840s, a steady stream of explorers moved west. And when gold was discovered in California in 1848, a flood of adventurers poured into the West from all over the world, uprooting Native Americans and Spanish-speaking people and changing the landscape of the country forever.

Between 1840 and 1860, more than a quarter of a million pioneers crossed America in wagons, on horseback, or on foot. Thousands more came by ship from Europe, Asia, and South America. It was one of the largest human migrations in the world's history.

While Native Americans, Mexicans, and Californios called the West home, the new settlers saw it as a stage on which anything was possible. Some said you could pluck a gold nugget as big as your fist from a California river. You could raise the biggest peaches anyone had ever seen in the fertile soil of Oregon Territory. You could haul wagons loaded with goods down the Santa Fe Trail and come back with your pockets bulging with silver.

Many of the first arrivals in the West were men. For years, the majority of history books presented western history through their eyes. Now, we realize that women also played an essential role in the dramatic changes that swept the country during the nineteenth century. We need to hear their stories, too. Otherwise, we are drawing a family tree but leaving out our mothers, aunts, sisters, and grandmothers.

The North American West offered women unusual challenges and opportunities. Although they faced great hardships, many women who moved west discovered that the skills they had practiced in their homes back East were invaluable in the West. Some bachelors, as well as men who had left their wives behind, were willing to pay a small fortune to a woman who could iron their shirts, cook them a decent meal, or stitch up an ugly wound. In the West, women also dared to take on jobs that were usually thought of as "men's work." A woman could start her own business, run a hotel and restaurant, even drive a stagecoach or dig for gold.

The West offered some women true independence. In many territories beyond the Mississippi River, a woman could buy and sell land—something unheard of in the rest of the world. In those days, it was almost impossible for eastern women to leave a difficult marriage, but western laws made it easier for women to get a divorce. Women in western territories were also the first to earn the right to vote: Wyoming passed a women's suffrage law in 1869, and in Utah women could vote in 1896. (The United

*Women played an important role in the history of the West.*
*Here, two girls traveling through the Southwest enjoy a game*
*during a noon rest stop.*

States didn't enact the Nineteenth Amendment—giving all
women the right to vote—until 1920.)

Many women thrived in the freer, more open life the West
offered. The eight women profiled in this book are examples of
women who broke the rules held by "civilized society" in those
times.

Why choose these particular women? First, each is a woman
of remarkable achievement. In the nineteenth century, no one
expected a woman to venture into the frontier alone, let alone
become a doctor, policewoman, or photographer; form her own
theater company; or speak out about human rights—but these

women did. Their strength and determination allowed them to face challenges such as poverty, lack of education, and illness with great courage. Each was a heroine who shaped the West during the most dramatic period of its history.

The eight women came from very different backgrounds and cultures. One was born in poverty and moved west to seek her fortune, while another gave up a life of comfort to travel in the wilderness. Three came as children; two were Native American sisters, born on the prairie; one was a slave, forced to travel west against her will. Some settled in the growing cities; while others made their mark in tiny mining towns or wilderness settlements. Born into ordinary or even difficult circumstances, each woman grew up to lead an extraordinary life.

In picking the women for this book, I also chose those who had left written documents behind, or whose lives had inspired others to write about them. Since all these women lived before the invention of radio, tape recorders, or video cameras, I looked for their diaries, letters, speeches, and stories. I tracked down their writings in libraries, historical societies, and museums. I read old newspapers with pages so brittle they almost fell apart in my hands. I searched through diaries written by others who lived at the same time, looking for details about each woman's time and place.

When the women hadn't set their thoughts down on paper, or when their records had been lost, I had to rely on other sources. I found oral histories passed down from one generation to the next. I dug into court records and read letters written by people who knew the women. I spoke with historians, artists, and architects who have also researched their lives, and talked to the descendants of two of the women, listening in awe as they shared stories about their pioneer ancestors.

Pictures from the early West were difficult to find. Photography was still in its early stages when most of the eight women were active. In the 1840s, many people had never even seen a photograph. Cameras were big and awkward, and few people had their pictures taken. When they did, they had to sit very still. If they moved or smiled, the picture would become blurred. Even the most lively, active people seemed stiff and serious when they posed for a photographer. The eight women in this book gaze at us from images that are faded or torn, but their faces help us to understand their individual characters and personalities and to imagine the voices we will never hear.

The stories of these women span four generations when the West changed forever. Although most never met, their lives were sometimes connected by common threads. In a strange twist of fate, the first woman profiled, Susan Magoffin, met General Zachary Taylor, the war hero who was destined to become president, while she was traveling in Mexico. Kate Ryan, the final woman in this book, was carried to her grave in Canada eighty-five years later by Zachary Taylor's great-grandson.

In the end, re-creating the lives of eight pioneer women is like stitching a quilt together. I hope this patchwork of their words, interwoven with the fragile old photographs, the clippings, memories, and legends, allows these high-spirited women to come to life again. Each woman's legacy shines like a gold nugget in the dark waters of our past.

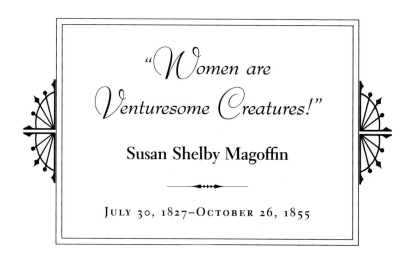

SUSAN SHELBY MAGOFFIN sat on the crest of a hill, writing in her diary. The thick woods around her carriage buzzed with activity as men prepared for the thousand-mile journey down the Santa Fe Trail.

Susan and her husband, Samuel Magoffin, were camped at Council Grove, west of Independence, Missouri. As Susan waited for their adventure to begin, huge hickory trees fell nearby, shaking the ground. Shavings flew while men shaped the green wood into spare axles and wagon tongues. "It is amusing to hear the shouting of the wagoners to their animals, whooping and hallowing," Susan wrote. "The cracking of their whips is almost deafening."

From that moment in June, 1846, when Susan began her journal, she marveled at her unusual situation. She was only eighteen years old, but she had already seen more of the country than most women her age. Soon after her marriage eight months

*Susan Magoffin in a daguerreotype taken when she was seventeen,
a year before she set off down the Santa Fe Trail*

before, she and Samuel had traveled east to Philadelphia and
New York to purchase the goods Samuel would sell in Mexico.
Now they were headed down the rugged Santa Fe Trail. "From
the city of New York to the Plains of Mexico is a stride that I
myself can scarcely realize," Susan wrote.

*Samuel Magoffin, Susan's husband, was a successful merchant, known and well-liked throughout Mexico.*

It was unheard of for an eastern woman to make the journey to Santa Fe, but pioneer life was in Susan's blood. Her great-grand-father, Isaac Shelby, had been a Revolutionary War hero and Kentucky's first governor. Susan's grandmother had survived bat-tles which took place near her home during the War of 1812. At a time when many Americans couldn't read or write, Susan had been educated by private tutors on her family's Kentucky farm. As she prepared for the trip, she had studied Spanish, to help her communicate with Mexicans along the way. She even gave her journal a Spanish title: *El Diaro de Doña Susanita Magoffin.*

Samuel Magoffin, Susan's new husband, had also grown up in Kentucky. Although he was twenty-seven years older, Susan was deeply in love with him. She referred to him, in her diary, as *mi alma* (my soul) or *mi querido* (my darling). She was also captivated by her husband's adventurous life: Samuel had traveled up and down the Santa Fe Trail for many years, trading goods to the Mexican people in exchange for silver. Yet he had never made the trip in such dangerous times.

While the Magoffins were loading their wagons, America had just declared war on Mexico. America's president, James Polk, had decreed that it was the "manifest destiny" of the United States to seize all the land between the Atlantic and Pacific Oceans. After Susan and Samuel crossed the Arkansas River, they would enter Mexican territory—and possibly, a war zone. In 1846, the land that now includes Texas, New Mexico, Utah, Colorado, Nevada, and California all belonged to Mexico.

Just behind the Magoffin's caravan, General Stephen Kearny was assembling an "Army of the West" to march on the town of Santa Fe. And Samuel's brother James was already a few days ahead of them, on a secret mission from President Polk. The president had asked James to negotiate with New Mexico's governor, Manuel Armijo. Polk hoped Armijo would cede his vast territory to the United States. If James were captured, all the Magoffins, including Susan, could be held as spies.

Although she knew of these dangers, Susan's diary rarely

showed any fear. While their caravan set off across the prairie, she held her large, calfskin book in her lap, filling the pages with her neat handwriting. Day after day, she described the people she met, the places they stopped, and the wonders of the journey. "Oh, this is a life I would not exchange for a good deal!" she wrote.

Their caravan, Susan said, was "quite a force." The Magoffins traveled with nineteen other men, a herd of two hundred oxen, and fourteen heavy freight wagons loaded with valuable merchandise. Ten teams of oxen hauled each wagon full of the silks, cottons, furniture, books, tools, and hardware that the Magoffins would sell in Mexico. They planned to return home by ship after selling all their goods.

Susan and her husband were headed down the oldest two-way road in the West. For hundreds of years, men and women from the Osage and other Plains Indian tribes had left the imprints of their moccasins along its sandy track. In 1540, the Spanish explorer Coronado followed the Santa Fe Trail in his search for the mythical "Seven Cities of Gold." French fur traders had carried their pelts over this route, and in 1821, the first American wagons jolted through Raton Pass into Santa Fe. In 1846, the year Susan made her journey, American merchants hauled a million dollars worth of goods to Mexico, while Mexican wagons headed north with silver, buffalo hides, mules, and sheep.

Most women who crossed the country during the nineteenth century did the cooking and washing, collected wood or buffalo "chips" for the fire, lugged water from springs or rivers, and often drove the family wagon. But because Samuel was a wealthy merchant, Susan traveled in style. "It is the life of a wandering princess," she wrote.

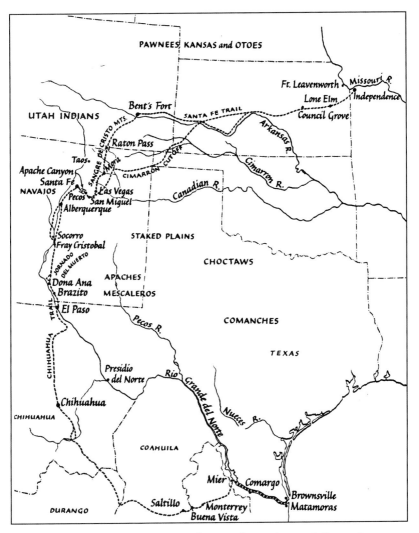

*Susan Magoffin's route from Independence, Missouri,*
*to Matamoras, Mexico*

Susan had a maid named Jane, three Mexican servants, and a loyal watchdog named Ring. She had her own private carriage as well as a saddle horse. She and Samuel slept in a cone-shaped tent complete with a table, folding chairs, camp stove, and carpet. Her only chores were making her own dresses and caring for her flock of chickens. Susan was amused by her situation. What woman "in civilized life," she wondered, "ever could [say] that the first house . . . to which my husband took me . . . was a tent?"

Since Susan had more leisure time than most travelers, she was able to keep up with her journal—often under difficult conditions. She wrote when she had to wear a thick veil to protect her face from the dusty desert wind. She wrote by firelight or at the noon hour when everyone else was resting. She wrote while mosquitoes beat against her canvas tent like a "hard rain." Their swarms, she decided, were "equal to any of the plagues of Egypt."

Susan recorded the sounds, smells, sights, and feelings of prairie life. "Last night I had a wolfish kind of a serenade!" she wrote one morning. Fortunately, her dog "flew out with a fierce bark and drove [the wolves] away."

A western artist, John Stanley, was traveling with their caravan. Susan often wished she could sketch prairie scenes as he did. Instead, she painted pictures with her words. When she met a Kaw Indian, she wrote that he wore nothing "but a breech clout [loincloth]. . . . He smoked his pipe while we were preparing dinner and watched us with a scrutinizing eye." She described the lush prairie grass, high enough "to conceal a man's waist," and the roses blooming near the door of her tent. As she wrote, Susan never guessed that one day her journal would become a unique record of southwestern history.

Susan also kept track of the hardships they encountered. As they reached the dry plains, there were few trees, water was scarce, and river crossings were hazardous. Coming down the steep banks of Ash Creek, Susan's carriage "whirled completely over with a perfect crash," leaving a "mess . . . of people, books, bottles . . . guns, pistols, baskets, bags, boxes . . ." Susan was thrown to the ground but wasn't hurt. On the trail to Bent's Fort, a thunderstorm lashed their tent and knocked it down. Susan called this disaster a "shipwreck on land." She and Samuel were buried in a tangle of canvas and poles, but again escaped unharmed. "As bad as it all is, I enjoy it still," Susan wrote.

On the dry prairie, the caravan passed huge wallows where the buffalo rolled in mud to protect themselves from mosquitoes and gnats. The buffalo, she decided, were "very ugly, ill-shapen things with their long shaggy hair over their heads, and the great hump on their backs." However, she enjoyed their meat, roasted over the fire.

Killing the buffalo put the traders in danger. The Kiowa, Comanche, and Apache Indians who lived in the area relied on the buffalo for their way of life. They used every part of the animal and resented the wasteful way some hunters took nothing but the buffalo's tongue after killing it. They were also angry when herds of oxen devoured the scarce grass, leaving little for the buffalo to eat. When Samuel went out on a buffalo hunt, Susan waited anxiously. "I am so uneasy from the time he starts until he returns," she wrote. Luckily, their caravan passed through without facing an attack.

In this same region, one of the Mexican men in Susan's caravan died of tuberculosis. "The grave is dug very deep, to prevent the body from being found by the wolves," she wrote. "The Mexicans always put a cross by the grave." Susan was concerned about her own health, for she began to mention visits from a French doctor who was also traveling to Santa Fe. Although she didn't confide this secret to her diary, Susan was pregnant.

Pregnancy never slowed her down. In those times, it was considered "unladylike" for women to go exploring on their own. In addition, women's long skirts and petticoats were confining, but Susan was having too much fun to behave in a "proper" way. One morning, she and her maid, Jane, went off to collect wild plums. They slid down the bank and cut long walking sticks to help them scale the steep trail on the other side. "Women are venturesome creatures!" Susan wrote afterward.

In early August, the Magoffins reached Bent's Fort, a fur-trading post on the Arkansas River. Susan moved into a room inside the fort's thick adobe walls. Just after her nineteenth birthday, she lost her baby. "In a few short months I should have been a mother and made the heart of a father glad," she wrote sadly.

Susan lay in bed mourning her loss and listening to the din outside. General Kearny's "Army of the West" had also reached the fort. Before long, she was well enough to pick up her journal again. "The shoeing of horses, neighing and braying of mules, the crying of children, the scolding and fighting of men, are all enough to turn my head." Although Susan was still weak, Samuel wanted the army's protection when he crossed into Mexican territory, so Susan was forced to climb back into the wagon when Kearny was ready to move on.

She recovered quickly. On the far side of the Arkansas River, she wrote, "I am entirely out of 'The States' and into a new country." Within a week, they entered the dreaded Raton Pass. One Sunday morning, while the rest of the caravan rested, Susan and Jane scaled a mountain. "What a magnificent view I had!" Susan remembered. She marveled at the "deep valleys below that looked blue. . . . The clouds seemed resting on the mountains around us."

On the other side of the pass, the caravan emerged onto a dry plain with snowy peaks in the distance. They met three *rancheros*

## STUCK FAST

*A pioneer's drawing of a mountain crossing. The Magoffin caravan faced similar perils in Raton Pass.*

(Mexican cowboys) and drew into the tiny town of Las Vegas, New Mexico. Here, Susan was surrounded by Mexican children and their parents, pushing and crowding to see the American woman in her bonnet. Mexican women, wrapped in wide, colorful scarves called *rebozos*, praised Susan's Spanish and offered her *cigarritas* as well as her first Mexican meal: tortillas and chili.

Before she left home, Susan had been told that Mexican people were "half barbarous." She disagreed. She enjoyed meeting these strangers, admired their children, and made an effort to speak their language. "They are certainly a quick and intelligent people," she said. "They are decidedly polite, easy in their manners, perfectly free, etc."

As they approached Santa Fe, the Magoffins received word that Samuel's brother James had accomplished his mission. Governor Armijo had fled New Mexico, and General Kearny had taken possession of Santa Fe without firing a single shot. Kearny's soldiers raised the American flag over the Palace of Governors in the town plaza.

On the night of August 30, 1846, a little more than two months after leaving Missouri, Susan walked into Santa Fe. "I have entered the city in a year that will always be remembered by my countrymen; and under the 'star-spangled banner' too," she wrote. The next phase of her adventures had begun.

Susan was thrilled to move into an adobe house, which she fixed up while Samuel sold his goods nearby. Within a few days, the Magoffins were receiving visitors. James Magoffin feasted with them on oysters and champagne. A Comanche chief called on Susan and they chatted in English and Spanish. Susan's Mexican neighbors invited her to an elegant ball where she watched her new friends dance the *cuna* to the tune of a guitar and violin. Although their governments were at war, the people of Santa Fe made the Magoffins feel at home.

Army officers also visited, including General Kearny. He

brought Susan news of troop movements, which she recorded in her diary. Susan reviewed the army's artillery with the general and admired his "splendid bay charger." When Kearny's army left for California in October, Susan grew restless. Hearing a rumor that "peace has been made," the Magoffins decided to continue south. Susan looked forward to exploring more of Mexico. Within a few days, she wrote, "Lo, we are camping again! And after all it is quite as good as staying in Santa Fe."

But the rumor of peace was false. Soon after they left Santa Fe, an express rider pulled into camp with news. A large Mexican force was "coming up from Chihuahua to take us," Susan wrote. In spite of this alarm, Susan went off on her own the next day. "I've had a real tramp this morning, through the mud, slipping down the riverbank, jumping the *saquia* [ditch] which . . . is quite a feat." She waded out to a sandbar in the Rio Grande, so that she could tell her family, when she returned home, that she had stood in the "wild deep murmur of a mighty river."

The Magoffins escaped an attack this time, but they continued to worry about being caught up in the war. Still, Samuel sold goods to villagers along the trail, while Susan made friends and soaked up Pueblo and Mexican culture. "I am so inquisitive," she wrote, "for I see so many new and strange ways of making everything. I always ask something about it."

In the late fall, the Mexican and American armies agreed to an uneasy truce and the Magoffins stayed with a kind family in San Gabriel for a few months. Susan spent her first wedding anniversary learning how to grind corn on a wet *mola* stone. She asked for recipes for Mexican dishes, which she said were "so fine, 'twould be a shame not to let my friends have a taste of them."

War broke out again in January. The Magoffins waited anxiously for Colonel Alexander W. Doniphan to arrive with another branch of the American army. (General Kearny had ordered all traders to travel with Doniphan, for their safety and to keep their supplies from falling into the hands of the enemy.) Then, at the end of the month, Susan heard terrible news that "started us from the village in haste. . . . The Taos people have risen and murdered every American citizen in Taos, including the governor." The Mexican army was also on the march.

"We are flying," Susan wrote. Ahead lay the dreaded desert known as the Jornada del Muerto (Journey of the Dead Man). "I wonder if I shall ever get home again?" she wrote. They crossed the desert in the dark. "The wind blew all evening, and the dust was considerable," Susan said. Even worse, the grass caught fire near their wagons when they stopped to eat. The men "beat it out with blankets" and the party moved on.

By mid-February, they were safely boarded with the family of a local *cura* (priest). As bloody battles raged in the mountains nearby, Susan struggled with her feelings. On the one hand, she agreed with a Mexican friend that Americans should never "invade the territory of another nation." Susan was very fond of her Mexican friends and grateful for all their kindness. "I can't help loving them," she wrote.

At the same time, she worried about her safety and feared for Samuel's life, wondering if she would be "torn from the dearest object to me on earth, perhaps both of us murdered." When she heard that the Americans had defeated the Mexicans at Buena Vista and then Sacramento, she kept her excitement hidden. She didn't want to offend her hosts.

The American army moved on to Chihuahua and the Magoffins followed them "over the worst roads I ever saw in my life,"

*The Magoffins fled before the Mexican army as it advanced on
Buena Vista, in the Sierra Nevada mountains.*

Susan wrote. In the shadow of the massive Sierra Madre range,
they traveled at night for safety, covering as many as thirty-five
miles a day, "jolting over stumps, stones, and ditches, half asleep,
expecting an attack from Mexicans constantly." To make things
worse, Susan was pregnant again. "I do think a woman *embara-
zada* [pregnant] has a rough time of it," she wrote in a rare com-
plaint. "This thing of marrying is not what it is cracked up to be."

In Saltillo, they were told that the Mexican government would
capture all traders and treat them as spies. The Magoffins cleaned
and loaded their guns—but once again, the attack never came.

By the end of the summer, the Magoffins reached Monterrey, where Susan met General Zachary Taylor. Taylor was a war hero, thanks to his defeat of the Mexicans in Monterrey the summer before. His nickname was "Old Rough and Ready," and one of his soldiers had written that he "looked like an old farmer going to market with his eggs." Susan agreed. "The general was dressed in his famed old gray sack coat, striped cotton trousers, blue calico neck-kerchief." Still, she said, "most of the wild stories I've heard of him I now believe false." She pronounced him "affable and altogether agreeable." Little did Susan know she had just called on the future president of the United States!

Leaving Monterrey, Susan and Samuel pushed on to the Gulf Coast. While distant battles around Mexico City brought an end to the war, Susan was camped out in the tiny town of Mier, "the most miserable hole imaginable." Strangers slept on the floor around her, but Susan took out her journal for one last entry to describe the fighting she had witnessed earlier in the day.

Susan's good luck ran out when she reached the Gulf of Mexico. She came down with yellow fever in the town of Matamoras just before she gave birth to a son, who died a few days later. Susan must have been devastated, but we can only guess at her feelings. She never touched her journal again.

Susan Magoffin recorded a war that few American journalists were able to witness or write about. In the 1840s, photography was just beginning, and few people had heard about the recent invention of the telegraph. Instead, they relied on diaries, letters, and other firsthand accounts to learn about important events. Susan's diary is a unique document. It contains valuable information about soldiers and battles, as well as the daily lives of people who were caught in the conflict. If Americans had been

*The war hero General Zachary Taylor, known as "Old Rough and Ready." Taylor later became America's twelfth president.*

able to read Susan's journal when she came home, they might have had a different view of the people they thought of as their enemy. And they would have learned valuable lessons about Mexico's history and customs.

Unfortunately, Susan died only eight years after leaving Mexico, and her diary lay forgotten for many years. It wasn't until the next century that historians could pore over Susan's careful entries to learn more about the period—and sometimes, to settle arguments about what really happened.

Reading Susan's account more than one hundred and fifty years after she started down the Santa Fe Trail, the reader steps back into the past. Thanks to the diary, we can smell the dust, taste the spicy chili, hear the whips cracking, and imagine the feelings of a woman who survived both a difficult journey and a war—and enjoyed almost every minute of it. As Susan herself wrote, "This is truly exciting times!"

---

*Soon after Susan Magoffin returned home, America signed a treaty with Mexico that ceded the present-day states of California, New Mexico, Utah, Arizona, Nevada, and Colorado to the United States. No one signing the treaty knew that nine days earlier, on January 24, 1848, someone had plucked a nugget of gold from the American River in California, starting a rush for wealth that would change the West forever.*

# "I'm a Star and That is Sufficient."

## Lotta Crabtree

NOVEMBER 7, 1847–SEPTEMBER 25, 1924

O N A DARK NIGHT IN 1854, a little girl named Lotta Crabtree huddled backstage, waiting for the music that signaled her entrance. She peeked out from behind the curtain, trying to see her audience. "The hall was full of miners," Lotta recalled. "There were candles for footlights, and the room smelled strongly of tobacco smoke."

Mart Taylor, owner of the saloon in Rabbit Creek, California, announced Lotta's entrance. The miners sat on the edges of their chairs. They were starved for entertainment and eager to see a child performer. But Lotta was terrified. She was only eight years old. Her biggest performance before this night had been in a blacksmith shop where she had danced on an anvil for a small group. Her mother gave her a firm nudge and then, Lotta remembered, she "stepped bravely out."

She wore a green coat, vest, and knee breeches, like a lepre-

*J. D. Borthwick's drawing of a gambling saloon, typical of the places where Lotta Crabtree's career began*

chaun. A tall green hat was perched on her red curls. She danced a jig, then a reel, and the crowd, full of Irish miners, went wild. Hurrying backstage, Lotta changed into a low-necked dress and came back to sing a sweet, sad song called "How Can I Leave Thee?" The miners wept, applauded, and showered her with Mexican and American coins, and gold nuggets—including a fifty-dollar slug! Lotta's mother, Mary Ann Crabtree, rushed onto the stage and scooped up their new wealth in a shoe.

Lotta earned more money that evening than most miners— including her own father—could make standing in an icy river

all week long, panning for gold. Lotta's long and wildly successful stage career had begun.

Lotta Crabtree was born in New York City in November of
1847, just two months before a small nugget of gold was found
in California's American River. She was only a year old when
news of the gold discovery was published in a special edition of
the *New York Herald*—too young to understand why thousands
of Americans came down with "gold fever" and stampeded off
to California.

Lotta's father, John Crabtree, ran an unsuccessful bookstore in
New York. He loved to wander near the harbor, where a tangle
of masts as thick as a forest rose from ships being loaded for California. Before long, as Lotta's mother remembered, "Nothing
would do but Crabtree [as she called him] must leave New York
to dig for gold in California. He never got any." When Lotta
waved good-bye to her father in 1851, no one could have predicted that the little girl with red hair and black eyes would be
the only Crabtree to strike it rich in the diggings.

Within a year, John Crabtree sent for his family. Mary Ann
gave up a profitable career as a seamstress, as well as her own private dreams of becoming an actress, to follow her husband. She,
too, had become infected with "gold fever."

Today, travelers to the West Coast can hop on an early flight
in New York and arrive in San Francisco by noon the same day.
Back then, the shortest route to the goldfields was by way of the
Isthmus of Panama. Lotta and her mother sailed on a steamship
from New York to Colón, Panama, where they boarded the
world's most expensive railroad, a line that ended in the jungle.
There, Mary Ann and her daughter climbed into a dugout canoe

paddled by Panamanians, rode thirteen miles to the Pacific coast on the back of a mule, then finally caught another steamer to San Francisco.

Three months after they left home, Lotta and Mary Ann arrived in San Francisco. The harbor was choked with abandoned ships whose crews had all scattered for the mines; the rough town was exploding into a city virtually overnight. Rats roamed the dusty streets, where new arrivals lived in tents or shacks. Miners poured into the city from the diggings, their pockets bulging with gold dust, looking for entertainment. Famous actors from all over the world were performing on makeshift stages set up in saloons and gambling halls.

As Lotta rode up the steep hills on her mother's arm, her red curls and infectious laugh made heads turn. Mary Ann Crabtree had always loved the theater, and she noticed right away that San Franciscans were captivated by child actors. Children as young as three or four were playing Shakespeare and drawing huge crowds. Lotta had inherited her mother's ability to sing and imitate almost anyone. Maybe she could become a child star, too. As soon as Mary Ann found John Crabtree in the town of Grass Valley, she signed Lotta up for dancing lessons.

In the summer of 1853, when Lotta was five, the Irish dancer Lola Montez moved to Grass Valley with her pet bear cub. Montez was known for her "Spider Dance," considered shocking because she lifted her skirts high at a time when most women didn't even show their ankles. The dancer made friends with the Crabtrees and taught Lotta some new songs and dances, including the fandango and the Highland fling.

Mary Ann's dreams of fame had shifted from herself to her daughter. "I made [Lotta] practice on our own broad hearthstone,"

*Lotta (kneeling), her mother, Mary Ann, and younger brother Jack pose for a photographer in San Francisco.*

Mary Ann remembered. "She could do a jig or a fancy dance, and had learned from me a ballad."

Soon, Mary Ann formed a small song and dance company with Mart Taylor, the owner of the tavern where Lotta had first performed. With Lotta as the star, Taylor on the banjo, and Mary Ann playing tambourine, they toured the mining camps. Little settlements with names like Bear Creek, Rough and Ready, and Port Wine offered "theaters" in canvas tents with curtains made from tattered blankets. The stages were just Lotta's size: wooden planks set across sawhorses, or two pool tables pushed together.

Traveling from one tiny camp to another was treacherous. Narrow trails, slick with mud, climbed up out of ravines, then dropped in stony switchbacks to the next river valley. But Lotta didn't mind. After each night's performance, she remembered, "I was often tied to the back of a mule, the man ahead taking the halter. I slept sweetly as our party jogged along." Years later, she said her earliest years in the mines were "Romantic! Romantic!"

The only thing that frightened Lotta was stepping onstage. She suffered from stage fright before every performance, and always relied on her mother to push her onstage. Once she faced the audience, Lotta relaxed and her eyes danced as fast as her feet. She was also a born comedian. She made up her own jokes, including a favorite where she flourished a tall stovepipe hat with its top cut off. Holding the hat out to the crowd at the end of every show, she looked astonished when gold nuggets and coins fell through the hat onto the stage. The miners howled with laughter—and tossed her even more money. "She was proclaimed the pet of the miners," one gold digger recalled.

Eventually, Lotta became so popular in the diggings that miners often escorted her out of town on their shoulders. But this success wasn't enough for Mary Ann. She wanted her daughter to perform on a real stage—and not just in any old theater. Mary Ann was determined that Lotta would appear at Maguire's Opera House, the grandest and most popular theater in San Francisco.

So in 1856, Lotta, her parents, and her two little brothers, Jack and George, left the mines for the city.

San Francisco had changed. Touring companies and famous actors from around the world—including the Booth brothers, Junius and Edwin*—had arrived to perform in a host of elegant theaters, which were being built as fast as they could be filled. (The American Theater, constructed in just twenty-five days, sank a few inches into the ground when the audience sat down on opening night!)

Lotta started from scratch again, and her first performance was a disaster. The audience was in an angry uproar about the play that had preceded her act. The crowd stomped their feet and shouted at the management while Lotta tried to sing. She soon grew hoarse and ran into the wings in tears.

But Mary Ann wouldn't let Lotta give up. She arranged for her to perform in small theaters called "melodeons," where the admission price was only a quarter. Melodeon crowds were rough, and Mary Ann made the other actors promise not to swear in front of her daughter. Melodeon actors were expected to act many parts, play an instrument, and sing, so Lotta took voice lessons and learned to play the banjo and the snare drum.

In the melodeons, Lotta faced competition from other child actors. A little girl named Jennie Worrell made her life especially miserable. Jennie's father had fitted boxes full of bullets into the heels of his daughter's shoes. When Jennie danced, the bullets rattled like a drumroll, making it seem as if she danced twice as fast as Lotta. Lotta's feet flashed and kicked, but the audience

---

* A third brother, John Wilkes Booth, would assassinate President Abraham Lincoln in 1865.

cheered louder for Jennie, and Lotta collapsed, weeping, in her dressing room after every performance.

But she grew more confident and overcame these obstacles. Lotta developed her own unique style. She was always daring onstage, breaking the rules for so-called respectable girls and women. She sprinkled her red hair with cayenne pepper to make it glitter in the spotlight and began playing boys' parts. (Boys' roles allowed her to wear knickers and clogs, which gave her more freedom when she danced.)

Lotta was flat chested and small for her age, and when she tucked her hair up under her hat and stuffed her hands into her pockets, she looked just like an Irish street urchin or the young newsboys and orphans who were as loyal as her fans in the mines. She was creating roles she would play all her life, such as a ruffian lost on the street, an orphan waif who searches for her parents, or the poor child who rises from rags to riches.

When Lotta first began to play boys' roles, her mother was upset by her boyish mannerisms. One night, Lotta reached for her pockets and discovered that Mary Ann had stitched them closed. Lotta was so upset, she ran offstage in tears. The next night, her mother gave in and let her daughter tuck in her hands and saunter across the stage as usual.

When Lotta did play a female role, she sat on a table and swung her feet, her skirts pulled up to her knees, shocking—yet thrilling—her audience. She enjoyed playing tricks on her fellow actors: Once, she smeared a woman's hair with real molasses instead of stage makeup and laughed as loudly as the audience when the actress's fingers stuck to her gooey curls. She also developed a unique way of saying good-bye at the end of a performance. As one theater critic wrote, "One of her favorite tricks . . .

was to extend a slim, dainty limb through the folds of the curtain and stamp her heel. . . . Lotta knew, as did everyone else, that her ankles were exceedingly pretty."

Lotta's life was unusual in many ways. She never had time to be a normal child. She rarely went to regular school (her longest stretch was six months, when she was thirteen), and her performances began late in the evening and continued long after midnight, so she didn't have time to make friends with other children. And Lotta's mother was always at her side, both backstage and at home. Mary Ann was small, but fierce. Dressed in black taffeta, her stern gaze scared many admirers away. A San Francisco neighbor, J. H. P. Gedge, had a crush on Lotta. Every day, he picked her the prettiest rose he could find. "I'd wrap it carefully and throw it into her back yard after dark," he said, "for if her mother saw the act, woe to me!"

While most children her age went to school or earned spending money doing odd jobs, Lotta supported her whole family from the time she was twelve. Her mother took charge of her earnings and insisted that Lotta be paid in cash, which Mary Ann lugged from the theater in a heavy leather bag. (In later years, when she and Lotta toured the country, this same bag would be filled with gold watches, diamonds, silver dollars, and trinkets showered on Lotta by fans.)

Lotta was thirteen when the Civil War broke out, and she still had not made it onto San Francisco's big stages. She went back to the diggings for a while, playing a Union drummer boy. In most places, her audiences rose with patriotic cheers when she strutted onstage with her drum, but in Roseburg, Oregon, she faced a crowd of newly arrived southerners who broke into rebel yells the instant they spotted her blue uniform. They

*Lotta as a teenager playing "The Little Drummer Boy," a soldier in the Union Army*

hissed and booed louder than Lotta could sing. Fearing for their lives, Lotta and her troupe slipped out the stage door and disappeared into the darkness.

Usually, Lotta stood up to danger. One night, her company

was crossing the swollen American River in a stagecoach. Lotta's banjo teacher, Jake Wallace, was driving. As the horses struggled through water up to their shoulders to pull the coach across the bridge, Lotta's mother and the other passengers cowered inside. Lotta leaned out the window and called, "Stay with 'em, Jake! Stay with 'em!" The horses floundered across and when Lotta looked back, she saw that the bridge had been swept down the river behind them. Lotta never flinched.

"She was a little mite of a thing," Jake Wallace said, "but she had sand and ginger enough for a dozen people."

When Lotta was fifteen, she finally broke into San Francisco's big stages by performing at a firemen's benefit. The audience gave Lotta a standing ovation as she sang "Rally Round the Flag, Boys," dressed in Union army blues. They cried when she crooned "Dear Mother, I'll Come Home Again." The fire company raised lots of money, and soon bigger theaters were clamoring for Lotta. She finally achieved her mother's dream: playing at Maguire's Opera House.

As her career took off, Lotta became friends with a famous older actress named Adah Menken. Menken took Lotta horseback riding, taught her to smoke the thin black cigars that became her trademark, and tempted her with stories about the bright lights of New York City. Mary Ann agreed with Menken: Lotta must perform on Broadway. After one last show at Maguire's Opera House, Lotta and her family left for the East.

Lotta crossed the Isthmus of Panama again, just as she had as an unknown child of five. Now she was seventeen and known all over California as "Our Lotta." In San Francisco, people hummed her most popular song, "The Captain with His Whiskers Gave a Sly Wink at Me." What would happen in New York, where no one had ever heard her name? Being Lotta, with a determination as fierce as her mother's, she decided she'd give it a try.

Breaking into New York's theater world was the toughest challenge Lotta ever faced. Her first performance was a flop, and soon Lotta and her family were on the road again, riding dusty, crowded trains instead of mules, staying in cheap hotels rather than tents. The work was grueling: Lotta often played six or seven parts in one show and performed in a different play each night. She stayed as fit and strong as an Olympic gymnast so she could swing across a stage on a rope or carry actors heavier than herself offstage.

"Lotta has been measured for the role, and it fits her to the knee," one critic wrote. "She prances up and down the stage sideways . . . or she jumps upon a table and won't keep quiet, although the thing rocks." This same writer added, "Lotta owes everything to nature and very little to art."

But her audiences didn't care. Lotta was drawing huge crowds again, and she took New York by storm, playing the title role in *Little Nell and the Marchioness*, a play written just for her. Before each performance, Lotta worked herself into the part of the sickly Nell by pacing her dressing-room floor, saying to herself: "I am very ill. I shall die soon. Serious! Serious!"

Lotta went on to become one of the most successful performers in the country. By the time she was twenty-one, she was earning more money than any other actress—and giving much of it away. Lotta was the first actress to travel with her own company, which rented its own railroad car. As always, Mary Ann set strict rules: Women must ride at one end of the car; men (including Lotta's brothers) at the other. When they stayed in hotels, Mary Ann stood guard outside Lotta's door, to protect her from her fans.

*Lotta as "Little Nell," from the play* Little Nell and the Marchioness, *one of her most successful roles*

Yet Lotta never complained about her mother. "Three things in my life have never disappointed me," Lotta wrote, "my mother, my public, and my sleep." Until she retired, Lotta depended on Mary Ann to help her overcome her stage fright. Watching Lotta run onstage brandishing two pistols, no one suspected that she still relied on her mother to give her courage before a performance and to help her memorize her lines. Years later, Lotta wrote a friend, "My mother has been all the world to me. . . . What is life, without a mother?"

As Lotta toured the country, playwrights clamored to create characters suited to her playful, brassy personality. Fans danced to the "Lotta Polka." Critics called her "a western wonder," "a canary bird," "a sparkling ingot." With her name pasted in big letters on theater marquees, Lotta boasted about her fame. "I am a continual success wherever I go," she wrote to a friend. "Your heart would jump with joy to see the respect I am treated with here. . . . I'm a star and that is sufficient."

In spite of her success, Lotta never forgot her most loyal fans. She was always faithful to miners, returning to tiny mining camps well into her forties. And wherever she traveled, Lotta saved the inexpensive seats in the pit, right below the stage, for boys who earned small wages delivering newspapers, shining shoes, or running errands in hotels. Although playwrights begged her to take on more serious parts, she refused. She knew her most popular roles were silly, but she didn't care. That's what her fans wanted—and Lotta loved her fans. "The public was as good as gold," she said. "Indeed, it *was* gold!"

Lotta grew up with the West. A pioneer since childhood, she shared the West's recklessness and bold spirit with audiences in rough taverns, Broadway theaters, and European opera houses.

She was ahead of her time—and yet, in some ways, she never grew up. Her mother forced her to perform in childish costumes until she was well into her thirties. For years, Lotta traveled the road with no home of her own, but she insisted, in the end, "I do not look back to the wandering life I led . . . with a bit of regret."

Lotta made her last public appearance before a crowd in her beloved San Francisco, when she was sixty-eight. The city was celebrating "Lotta Crabtree Day." Lotta arrived in a stagecoach pulled by white horses and stepped out near the fountain she had built for the city's thirsty dogs and horses. There, she was greeted by brass bands, choirs, and thousands of cheering admirers. "Dear friends," Lotta began, "this is the most sincere and significant tribute given to any woman in the world—"

Her voice broke. She wanted to thank her mother—now dead—and her loyal fans everywhere, but she couldn't speak. She began to weep.

"LOTTA! LOTTA! LOTTA!" the crowd cried.

It was the biggest audience she'd ever faced. Even in silence, she held them in the palm of her hand.

◆•••◆

*While thousands of prospectors, like the Crabtrees, rushed to California to seek their fortunes, others were forced to make the long and hazardous journey against their will—yet they still left their mark on the West.*

# "For the Sum of Love and Affection and Ten Dollars"

## Bridget "Biddy" Mason

———◆•••◆———

AUGUST 15, 1818–JANUARY 15, 1891

A COLD NOVEMBER WIND blew down from the mountains, chilling a sturdy black woman named Bridget as she picked her way along the stony trail. Carrying her infant, Harriet, under one arm, she herded the pioneers' sheep and cows while she worried over her two other daughters. Ahead of her, fifty-three Mormon travelers rode in the wagons that had carried them since they left Mississippi seven months earlier. But Bridget—or Biddy, as she liked to be called—had crossed the entire country on foot, caring for her three little girls as the wagon train lumbered over the prairie and climbed the Rocky Mountains. Forced to walk at the rear of the caravan for nearly two thousand miles, Biddy and her daughters choked on the dust churned up by the wagons.

The Mormon men and women ahead of Biddy had a mission: to reach the promised land they called Deseret (now Salt Lake

City, Utah). But Biddy was traveling against her will. She had been a slave since the moment she was born, thirty years earlier. She was owned by a man named Robert Smith, a Mormon convert and member of the caravan. Hannah, another slave, who trudged along next to Biddy, was having an even more difficult time: She was pregnant with her fifth child.

As the two women struggled to care for their young children, neither one could know that they would soon be involved in one of slavery's most famous court cases. And Biddy never dreamed that one day she would become one of the wealthiest and most generous women in Los Angeles.

Biddy's early life is a mystery. Her daughter believed that Biddy was born in Hancock County, Georgia. Other accounts list her birthplace as Mississippi. We don't know if Biddy was allowed to stay with her parents as she grew, or if she was sold to other owners, as happened to many slave children.

No matter who raised her, Biddy had been expected to work from a very young age. By the time slave children were three or four, they were doing simple chores such as feeding chickens, gathering eggs, or sweeping the yard. By the age of ten, most children labored in the fields alongside their parents. Biddy also knew how to care for livestock, so she was put in charge of the animals on the wagon train.

Although some slaves studied secretly in their cabins at night, they were forbidden to have a formal education. Biddy never learned to read or write and she signed her name with an X. But she had absorbed other important skills. Like many women born into slavery, Biddy was taught to help those who were in trouble and to look out for the people in her community. In addition, she was trained as a healer. From the time she was young, she

*The only known portrait of Biddy Mason*

took care of people who were sick or injured on the plantation. Biddy knew which plants and herbs would cure different illnesses. Her knowledge may have included information about African and Caribbean medicines, as well as healing herbs that were common in the South. These lessons were handed down on the plantations from one generation of women to the next.

As Biddy traveled west, she was expected to care for her owner's children when they were sick and to nurse their mother, Rebecca Smith, who was often ill. The other whites on the wagon train called on Biddy when they needed medical help, even though many Mormons believed that dark-skinned people were inferior.

Biddy also knew how to "catch babies," as people described the work of midwives who helped women in childbirth. Three Mormon women on Biddy's train gave birth between Mississippi and Utah, including one whose child was born on a stranded ferry. Biddy probably "caught" those babies, and she assisted Hannah when her new baby came.

Biddy and Hannah stayed in Utah Territory with the Smiths for three years before moving to San Bernardino, California. The Smiths wanted to start another Mormon community, so Biddy, Hannah, and their children followed the wagon train again, forced to cross the blistering Mojave Desert on foot.

It was 1851, and California had recently become a state. Biddy's owner didn't realize until after he arrived that the state's new constitution forbid slavery. Although there was great prejudice in California against all people of color (including Native Americans, African Americans, and Chinese), Robert Smith worried that if he stayed he might lose his slaves, so a few years later, he decided to take everyone to Texas, where slavery was still legal. At the start of their journey, Smith hid his party in a canyon in Santa Monica, near the Pacific Ocean. Hannah was pregnant with her eighth child, so perhaps Smith was waiting for her baby to be born before they left.

While they were hiding, Biddy realized that if she and Hannah were taken to Texas, they might be slaves forever. During her stay in San Bernardino, Biddy had made friends with the free black family of Winnie and Robert Owens. Robert was a successful rancher, horse trader, and businessman and his son, Charles, was in love with Biddy's daughter Ellen. Somehow,

Biddy sent a message to the Owens family about her plight. Charles rounded up some *vaqueros* (cowboys) from the family ranch and appeared in the canyon with the sheriff. They carried a legal document that put Biddy and Hannah's families "under charge of the Sheriff of this county for their protection."

Everyone was afraid that the Smiths would steal Biddy and Hannah away, so the sheriff locked the women and their children in the county jail during their trial. The jail was an adobe building with a leaky roof. Visitors to the courtroom sat under umbrellas while Biddy petitioned the judge for her freedom. Because people of color were not allowed to testify in court, Biddy could not speak on her own behalf. She and Hannah were represented by a lawyer who challenged Judge Benjamin Hayes of the Los Angeles District Court to uphold California's constitution.

Biddy's action took great courage. If she failed and was returned to Robert Smith, she and Hannah might be severely beaten, then forced to leave California against their will. Although Smith's lawyer knew Biddy had refused to leave with Smith, he insisted that Hannah and her children "were well disposed to remain with him." He then tried to bribe Biddy's lawyer, offering him a hundred dollars if he would give up the case.

Inside the jail, a guard overheard the two women discussing their fear of Smith. He told the judge, who met with Biddy and Hannah in his private chambers. Hannah was too afraid to speak, but Biddy was determined to plead her case. "I always feared this trip to Texas, since I first heard of it," she told the judge. "Mr. Smith told me I would be just as free in Texas as here."

Judge Hayes knew that Smith was lying to Biddy, since Texas was still a slave state. After considering all the evidence, he ruled that "all of the said persons of color are entitled to their freedom and are free forever." He also said, "Neither slavery nor involuntary servitude . . . shall ever be tolerated in this state." Robert Smith was ordered to pay the costs of the trial, but he never appeared in court. He and his wife had fled to Texas.

Biddy, Hannah, and their eleven children were free for the first time in their lives. It was January, 1856, nine years before the Thirteenth Amendment abolished slavery in America. Biddy's court case was written up as a landmark. The judge had advised Biddy and Hannah to "become settled and work for themselves—in peace and without fear."

Biddy was thirty-seven years old. She had no home, no job, and no husband to help her bring up her daughters.* But she had her Certificate of Freedom. She also had skills—and friends. Robert Owens and his wife, known as Uncle Bob and Aunt Winnie, lived in a comfortable frame house in Los Angeles surrounded by a picket fence. They opened their home to Biddy and her family.

Biddy started her new life by taking on a last name—Mason—and immediately found a job as a midwife and nurse. She worked for Dr. John Griffin, a friend of the Owens family, for $2.50 a day. Before long, her nursing and midwifery skills were in great demand. Biddy was doing the work she was trained to do, and she was earning her own money at last. She nursed Dr. Griffin's patients in the county hospital and all over the growing city.

It was not easy to be an African American in California in the 1850s. Even though the last Mexican governor of California, Pio

---

* There are no records to tell us who the father of Biddy's children was.

*Women from the Owens and Mason families on the front porch
of the Owens' home. Biddy and her children took refuge here
after gaining their freedom.*

Pico, had been a man of African descent, the new state turned
its back on people of color. Although African Americans paid
taxes, they couldn't vote, attend white churches, or enroll their
children in public schools.

Los Angeles was especially unfriendly for the few blacks who
lived there. (The census of 1860 listed only seventy African Americans in the region.) Many whites came to Los Angeles from
southern states, where they had often treated blacks cruelly. Rev-
erend John Brier, who lived in the city, described a raid on a
local hotel where southerners beat and tortured black residents
"just on a lark."

But people always needed Biddy's skills, and she was welcomed into many different homes in spite of the area's prejudice. She helped Californio women in luxurious adobe homes give birth, attended Native American women living in temporary shacks next to the citrus groves, visited white settlers on isolated ranches, and assisted at the births of African American babies in her own neighborhood.

When an expectant mother saw Biddy come through the door, carrying her heavy black midwife's bag, she must have felt relieved. One woman remembered that a midwife packed her bag with "everything she needed. . . . She had her scissors . . . that she cut the baby's cord [with] . . . and big number eight white spools of thread," as well as herbs and medicines to help the mother and her new child. Often, a midwife stayed on to help the family after the baby was born, preparing meals and teaching the mother how to care for her infant. Midwives were often called "Grandma" or "Aunty." Years later, Biddy's grandson Robert Owens recalled that she had been "known by every citizen" as Aunt Biddy.

Biddy ignored the dangers that came with being a healer. She risked her life by nursing people during a smallpox epidemic in the 1860s and treated rough prisoners at the county jail where she had been held during her court case.

After ten years of hard work, Biddy saved enough money to buy her own piece of land. Biddy was one of the first African American women to own property in California.* Her lot, which

* Nancy Gooch, a freed slave from northern California, bought Sutter's sawmill with her son after Sutter abandoned it. This was the site where gold was first discovered in 1848.

ran between Spring and Fort Streets (later Broadway), was on the outskirts of town. (The map of the area at that time was titled "A Map of the Plains.") The streets were unpaved and the only light in the evenings came from gas lamps lit by a young boy who rode from block to block at dusk, carrying a torch. Many residents had gardens. Biddy's daughter remembered, "There was a ditch of water . . . and a willow fence running around the plot." When she claimed the deed Biddy told her children, "This first homestead must never be sold."

At first, Biddy didn't live on her land. She continued to rent it, save her money, and buy up other properties. Biddy was a shrewd businesswoman who understood the value of real estate. After the Civil War, the city was growing fast. The transcontinental railroad was finished, linking San Francisco with the East. When the railroad reached Los Angeles, it brought thousands of new residents, and Biddy's properties quickly increased in value. For example, she bought four lots for $375 in 1868 and sold them for $2,800 just sixteen years later. In 1909, a story in the *Los Angeles Times* reported that Biddy's original Spring Street property "could not be bought for a quarter of a million dollars." By then, her lot was in the heart of downtown Los Angeles.

While Biddy's wealth grew, she lived simply and didn't flaunt her riches. Even when she finally moved into the brick building she had constructed on her Spring Street property, she stayed in the upstairs apartment and rented out the ground floor.

Biddy bought land so that her children and grandchildren could have a home base. She also knew that owning property could help them become self-sufficient. She deeded part of her homestead lot to her grandsons, Robert and Henry Owens, so they could start a livery stable. Many years later, when Robert

*By 1900, Biddy Mason's Spring Street lot was in the heart of downtown Los Angeles. (Her two-story building is on the bottom right, just before the "Niles Pease" sign.)*

Owens had become the wealthiest black man in the city, he credited Biddy with his success: "My grandmother . . . proved my salvation," Owens said. "She told my father that he could not make a farmer or a blacksmith out of a boy who wanted to be a politician, and she was right." Biddy's deed to her grandsons, signed with the X she called "her mark," read that the land was given "for the sum of love and affection and ten dollars."

In her time, Biddy Mason was most famous for the wealth she gave away. She was generous to everyone who needed help. When the city suffered severe flooding in the 1880s, Biddy went

*In 1989 the city of Los Angeles built this eighty-one-foot memorial
wall to honor Biddy Mason's life and achievements.*

to her local grocery store and set up a special account to send
food to all the homeless victims of the flood. In 1872, Biddy
called a meeting in her living room to found the First African
Methodist Episcopal Church. She paid its taxes for many years.
(This church is now one of the biggest and most prominent
African American churches in the city.)

The *Los Angeles Times* recalled that "In the slums of the city,
she was known as 'Grandma Mason'" and reported she was "a
frequent visitor to the jail, speaking a word of cheer and leaving
some token and a prayerful hope with every prisoner." Biddy is
also credited with having started a school and day care center

during the years when African American children—including her own—were not allowed to attend public schools.

Biddy's Spring Street home was known as a place of refuge. The door was open to people who needed help, as well as to African American settlers who had recently arrived in the area. When she was ill at the end of her life, the *Los Angeles Times* remembered, "It became necessary for her grandson to stand at the gate each morning and turn away the line which had formed, awaiting her assistance."

Biddy died at age seventy-two, one of the wealthiest women in Los Angeles. Although she left no written records behind, one of her sayings became an important legacy for her children, and for the people of her city. In the 1980s, nearly one hundred years after Biddy's death, her great-granddaughter Gladys remembered Biddy's words, passed on from one generation to the next:

"If you hold your hand closed . . . nothing good can come in. The open hand is blessed, for it gives in abundance, even as it receives."

———◆••◆———

*While California was a magnet for people seeking gold and instant wealth, pioneers in search of fertile farmland were drawn to the Pacific Northwest, then known as Oregon Territory. In Oregon, as in other parts of the West, there were new opportunities for adventurous women who thrived on the challenge of wilderness life.*

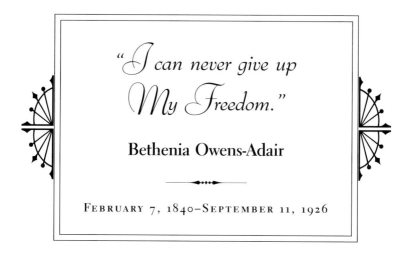

A STORM RAGED AROUND a farmhouse near Astoria, Oregon. Trees snapped, the wind shrieked, and the house trembled. Suddenly, lantern light flashed across the bedroom window. Dr. Bethenia Owens-Adair, who lay awake listening to the storm, threw on her clothes and ran to the door. A man stood outside, rain streaming from his shoulders. A woman in Seaside, fifteen miles away, had a bad infection and desperately needed a doctor. Could Bethenia come?

"You'll not go!" her husband called from the bedroom.

Bethenia was in her fifties, but she didn't hesitate, even though she'd never heard such a fierce wind. She was proud that in all the years she'd practiced medicine, she'd "never refused a call, day or night." Besides, she was the only doctor for miles around. She cut a hole in an old blanket, climbed onto her horse, and pulled the blanket over her head, cinching the corners to the saddle so the wind wouldn't blow her off. The messenger walked ahead of her, chopping at fallen trees with his ax to make a path for the doctor's horse. Seven hours later, exhausted and wet to the skin, they arrived at the sick woman's house. Bethenia opened the woman's infected wound, drained it, and covered it with a hot poultice. In those days before antibiotics, an infection could be life threatening if it wasn't treated, so Bethenia stayed until the next day to be sure her patient was safe.

"This was frontier life!" Bethenia wrote later. "Hard, strenuous, often dangerous."

Bethenia Owens was born in Van Buren County, Missouri, in 1840. When she was three years old, her family joined a wagon train headed for the rich farmland in the territory known as Oregon Country. Right from the start, Bethenia insisted on traveling at the front of the caravan, riding on Captain Jesse Applegate's shoulders. Applegate, a famous wilderness guide, was captivated by the lively girl with bright eyes who became his lifelong friend. "Fame and fortune await you," he told Bethenia.

Perched high on the captain's shoulders, Bethenia was too young to think about her future. She was enjoying the excitement of the journey. A line of wagons stretched behind her, snaking over the prairie under a dust cloud six miles long. In the distance, her father, Thomas Owens, chased a herd of buffalo while her brother, Flem, and sister, Diana, rode with their mother, Sarah, in the family wagon.

Traveling west in the 1840s was a more carefree adventure for the children than for the adults. On the Owens' train, storms soaked their precious sacks of cornmeal; men drowned at river crossings; oxen died of hunger; and the pioneers had to cut a trail through sagebrush six feet high. After shooting the rapids on the

*A mural on the Oregon State Capitol Building showing the
"Great Wagon Train of 1843," which brought Bethenia and
her family to Oregon*

Columbia River, Bethenia's bedraggled family finally arrived at
Tansy Point, Oregon. It was Christmas Day, 1843, eight long
months since they had left Missouri. They had lost their animals,
their wagon, and most of their belongings. Bethenia's father only
had a half-dollar in his pocket.

For months, the family had nothing to eat but salmon and
potatoes, and the children had no shoes. But Bethenia's parents
were resourceful. Thomas Owens built a log cabin and a grist-
mill. When spring came, Bethenia's mother planted a garden

and grew flax to make linen. She traded the strong fiber to Native American fishermen. They wove it into fishnets and gave her salmon, and deerskin for moccasins, in return.

The Owens family grew quickly, and eventually, Bethenia had eight brothers and sisters. Like all frontier children, Bethenia was expected to help with daily chores. "Boys and girls of fourteen or fifteen were expected to do a full day's work on the farm or in the house," Bethenia said later. She and Flem were still young themselves when they started caring for the smaller children. "When the weather was fine, we fairly lived outdoors, hauling the baby in its rude little sled, or cart, which bumped along," Bethenia remembered. If it rained, they played in the barn, where Bethenia said they would "slide down the steep hay-mow, from the top to the bottom." When her brothers and sisters cut themselves or bumped their heads, they always ran to Bethenia. "I was the family nurse," she said.

Bethenia learned her first nursing skills from her mother. Women physicians were unheard of in those days. (Bethenia was born nine years before Elizabeth Blackwell became the first woman in America to earn a medical degree.) Bethenia's mother had been known for her healing abilities since their trip across the country, when she nursed many sick pioneers. Like other frontier women, Sarah Owens knew how to make medicines from herbs in her garden, and she had probably learned from Oregon's Native Americans which plants could be used for healing. She passed her knowledge on to Bethenia, along with her belief that healthy food, lots of outdoor exercise, and plenty of rest were the keys to good health.

Except for learning these healing skills, Bethenia rebelled against the way girls were expected to behave. Her parents were understanding and let her help with outside chores instead of housework. "She is such a tomboy, I can never make a girl of her," Sarah Owens said. Bethenia's long braids flew as she hurried around the farm gathering eggs under the barn floor, feeding the animals, or weeding the garden. Her father often called her his "boy."

If only she *had* been born a boy! "It was the greatest regret of my life," Bethenia wrote later, "for I realized very early in life that a girl was hampered and hemmed in on all sides."

In spite of these words, Bethenia never behaved as if she were "hemmed in." She was always small, but described herself as "tough and active," boasting that she often got the best of her brother Flem in their friendly wrestling matches. "Not until I was past twelve did he ever succeed in throwing me," she said. When she was thirteen, she bet Flem she could carry two hundred pounds of flour across the kitchen—which she did by balancing the heavy sacks on her shoulders.

Bethenia was also proud of her abilities on horseback. Bethenia's next-door neighbor, a rancher named Miss Ann Hobson, taught her to ride a horse astride instead of sidesaddle, as "proper" ladies were expected to do. Miss Hobson would scoop Bethenia up onto her saddle and spur her horse to a gallop. "Away we would go like mad over the prairie," Bethenia said. Soon she was riding as fast as Miss Hobson on her own mare, Queen. She and Flem were such confident riders that their father let them drive his herd of Spanish cattle all the way across the state when Bethenia was only twelve.

In that same year, Bethenia went to school for the first time. A teacher, Mr. Beaufort, boarded with the Owens family and started a school. "I simply worshipped my handsome teacher," Bethenia said. When Mr. Beaufort taught her to read, Bethenia felt as if she had found "an oasis in the desert."

After a few months, Mr. Beaufort left for another town. Bethenia hid behind the house and cried. She had promised him she would "study her book hard." But how could she, with no teacher? Bethenia wouldn't go to school again for six long years.

In 1853, the Owens family moved to Roseburg, in southern Oregon, to find more pasture for their growing herd of cattle. The next year, Bethenia married Legrand Hill, a young man who had worked for her father on their first farm. She was only fourteen, and still so small she could stand under Legrand's outstretched arm. Her parents didn't object. At that time, many people treated girls Bethenia's age as if they were already adults. Bethenia arrived at her new home with her horse, Queen, her own milk cow and heifer calf, a wagon and harness, a feather bed, and seeds for the garden, which she planted the day she moved in. The unfinished cabin had a dirt floor and no stove or chimney. Snakes sunned themselves on the roof. In spite of this, Bethenia said, "I had high hopes for the future."

Bethenia fixed up her new home with her usual energy. "I was as active as a squirrel," she wrote later. She chinked the cabin with moss and mud to keep out the snakes and rodents and was soon selling her own butter and eggs. But Legrand didn't like to work. Even worse, when their son, George, was born, Legrand was cruel to the baby and often hit Bethenia. One night when George was two, Legrand forced him to eat six hard-boiled eggs, then threw him down on the bed. Bethenia scooped up her son and ran to the river where her brother Flem ferried them to safety.

Divorce was almost unheard of in those days, but Bethenia was determined to regain her independence. She went to court and won the right to keep her son and take back her family name. After her divorce she felt "like a free woman," yet she was only eighteen and responsible for George. How could she earn a living?

Bethenia had always believed that having an education was the key to success in life. Roseburg had a school, and George loved playing with his mother's younger brothers and sisters. Bethenia made a deal with her family: She would do all the washing and help with farm chores if they would watch George while she returned to school.

It was humiliating to sit in arithmetic classes with the youngest children. But Bethenia got up every morning at four to help her father in the barn, studied with the principal after school, and

*The schoolhouse that Bethenia Owens attended in Roseburg, Oregon, when she was eighteen—many years older than the other students*

propped her books on the ironing board at night after George was asleep. In four months, she passed difficult tests in spelling, arithmetic, geography, and reading.

For the next few years Bethenia lived and worked all over

Oregon. Her father offered to support her, but Bethenia refused. "No amount of argument would shake my determination to earn my own livelihood, and that of my child," she said. At first, she and George boarded with other families, often in exchange for Bethenia's doing their sewing and laundry. By day, Bethenia taught school. At night, her foot pumped the treadle of the sewing machine after she had prepared her lessons for the next day. "Work was scarcely more than play," she said. Eventually, she earned enough money to buy her own home, and to start her own hat-making business back in Roseburg.

Wherever she lived, Bethenia took on nursing jobs. Local doctors called on her to assist them with difficult cases, and neighbors often asked for her help with sick women and newborn babies. One night she stopped at a friend's house to help an older physician, Dr. Palmer, with a sick child. The doctor's sharp instrument slipped, and he cut the little girl's arm. When he stopped to wipe his glasses, Bethenia picked up the instrument. "Let me try, Doctor," she said. She dressed the wound, and was pleased that she brought "immediate relief to the tortured child." Dr. Palmer was furious at Bethenia for interfering.

Years later, Bethenia remembered this night as a turning point in her life. "A desire began to grow within me for a medical education," she said. Within a few days, Bethenia had stopped by the drugstore to borrow a copy of *Gray's Anatomy*. As she came outside, she ran into the lawyer who had helped her win her divorce many years before. He noticed the book and said, "Go ahead. It is in you. . . . You will win."

At that time, there were only a few medical schools in the West, and none accepted women. Bethenia studied the anatomy book in secret. In 1871, she sent George off to college and

*Bethenia as a young woman. Her hat may be one she made in her millinery shop.*

announced that she was going to Philadelphia to study medicine.

Her family was horrified. "I was not prepared for the storm of opposition," Bethenia wrote later. Her parents, her brothers and sisters, even George, all tried to change her mind. Men were smart enough to be doctors—but not women. How could she learn all that science? What about the blood and gore of surgery?

Just before Bethenia left for the East, one loyal customer ran into her hat shop and cried, "I am thoroughly disgusted! You must have lost your head!"

Bethenia was shaken, but she managed to stay calm. "I will come home in a few years and be your doctor," she said.

"No woman will ever doctor *me!*" the woman announced, and stomped out in a rage.

On the dark, windy night when Bethenia left Oregon, she carried a letter from her old friend Jesse Applegate, the wilderness guide who had hoisted her onto his shoulders nearly thirty years before. "The Creator designed you for a higher destiny," he wrote, "and you will attain it."

Bethenia wasn't so sure. Rain lashed the side of the stage-coach, in which she was the only passenger. As the horses strug-gled through the deep mud, Bethenia wept. "I was starting out in an untried world alone," she wrote later. "All I had left behind tugged at my heart strings." But then, she remembered, "Every great trouble in my life had proved a blessing in disguise." Hadn't she always made it, in spite of the obstacles in her way? She had educated herself, raised George without a penny of sup-port from his father, and been successful in business. Bethenia sat up straight. She was starting a new life, just as her parents had when they immigrated to Oregon. "My mind was made up," Bethenia said. "I would never turn back."

After study at the Eclectic School of Medicine and training at Blockly Hospital, both in Philadelphia, Bethenia returned to Roseburg, proudly carrying her first degree. Soon, word spread that six doctors were about to perform an autopsy on the body of an old man who had just died. Autopsies allowed doctors and medical students to understand how the body worked. They also provided gruesome entertainment—for men only.

Dr. Palmer, the physician whose clumsiness inspired Bethenia to become a doctor, invited her to attend the autopsy. He meant it as an insult, assuming she would never come. Instead, Bethenia answered, "I will be there in a few minutes." She hurried to the crude shed, opened the door, and found an audience of fifty men gathered to watch the doctors. The old man's body lay on a board, hidden under a gray blanket.

Dr. Palmer was shocked. "I object to a woman being present!" he roared, even though he had invited her himself. The five other doctors voted to let Bethenia stay, and Dr. Palmer stormed out. Another doctor handed Bethenia the scalpel and asked her to make the first cut, thinking she would refuse. Bethenia didn't hesitate. While the crowd jeered, she took the sharp knife and went to work.

News spread all over town that the "lady doctor" was cutting up a dead man. Writing her autobiography years later, Bethenia remembered that when she came out of the shed, "the street was lined on both sides with men, women, and children," all waiting to see "the woman who dared." Bethenia held her head up, although she knew she would have been run out of town if her brothers hadn't lived there. They might be ashamed of her, but they would never let anyone harm their sister.

In a short time, Bethenia sold her hat-making shop, packed

her things, and moved to Portland, where she established a busy practice. Even her former hat customer who had vowed she'd never see a woman doctor traveled all the way from Roseburg for an appointment.

Bethenia wasn't satisfied, however. Her first level of training had prepared her to be only a "bath doctor," using special medicated baths, operated by electricity, to ease the pain of arthritis and rheumatism. So Bethenia started saving money again. After she earned enough to send her sister to college and George to medical school, she enrolled in the University of Michigan, one of the first medical schools in the country to accept women. This time, even Jesse Applegate tried to persuade her to stay home. Perhaps she could marry again? Bethenia didn't listen. "I can never give up my freedom, my individuality," she said.

Bethenia was thirty-eight when she entered the university. As always, she had the energy to rise at four in the morning for "a cold bath followed by vigorous exercise." She studied sixteen to eighteen hours a day in classrooms where men and women were separated by a curtain so they couldn't see one another. But Bethenia was learning real medicine at last. Now she could deliver babies, perform operations, diagnose patients with many different illnesses, and prescribe the right medicines—all the skills she'd longed for when she was young and traveling from farm to farm to help sick women and their children.

In June of 1880, brass bands played as Bethenia and her classmates marched onto the university green to receive their diplomas. After a year of further study in Europe, Bethenia returned to Portland by ship. In her pocket, she carried letters from Oregon's governor and senators, welcoming her home. At age forty, she was *Doctor* Bethenia Owens at last—the first woman physi-

*Downtown Portland, Oregon, at the time Dr. Bethenia Owens opened her medical practice. Even heavy rains and floods couldn't keep her from visiting patients.*

cian in the Pacific Northwest. She had achieved the fame that Jesse Applegate had once predicted.

Bethenia had been single for twenty-two years while she raised her son and pursued her career. Soon after she set up her medical practice, she married Colonel John Adair, a cheerful childhood friend. Unlike her first, difficult husband, Bethenia wrote, "There were no dark shadows in his pictures, and my love for him knew no bounds."

The Adairs had a daughter, who died after only three days. A few years later, they adopted Mattie, the orphaned daughter of a patient, and took in Bethenia's grandson, John, when his mother died. For many years, they lived on a farm in northern Oregon, a place so remote that Bethenia sometimes rode her horse thirty miles to see patients.

Bethenia never lost her energy or her love for adventure. The day she retired, she hitched up her horse for a drive to the headwaters of the Columbia River. There, she would shoot the rapids in a boat again, just as she had as a child. Colonel Adair and her friends thought she was too old to travel alone, but Bethenia ignored their worries. "I have never flinched from any undertaking," she said, "and I hope I never shall!"

---

*After the first rush to the West Coast, pioneers began to move onto the prairies and plains, which had been opened to settlement by the federal government. The settlers ignored the fact that these lands already belonged to the native tribes who had lived there for centuries—and who now found their livelihood and way of life endangered.*

A LITTLE GIRL STOOD outside the Sacred Tent, waiting for the ceremony to begin. She was barely old enough to walk on her own, yet her grandmother, Nicomi, told her she must enter the big tent all by herself. In the ceremony called the Turning of the Child, the elders would give the girl her adult name. And because she was the daughter of Iron Eye, the Omaha chief, she must go first.

Mary, the child's mother, called out to the spirit of the Sacred Pole, asking him to receive her daughter, then released her little girl's hand. The child took a few shaky steps forward, clutching her new moccasins. Suddenly, the priest emerged from beneath the tightly stitched skins of the tent. The feathers and fur of his headdress loomed over her. The child screamed and tried to run away but Nicomi caught her and shoved her firmly forward. No one disobeyed Nicomi. The child took a deep breath and stepped inside.

The tent flap was open to the east. The priest set the child on a smooth stone, then lifted her to the four points of the compass. A high-pitched song floated out over the bluffs. The priest slipped her feet into the new moccasins and gave her the name that fixed her place in the tribe: Inshta Theumba, or Bright Eyes. She took four careful steps in her new shoes, as the priest instructed, then ran to her mother and grandmother, her black eyes shining.

This Omaha ceremony was held to start each child on the journey of life. No one seated outside the tent could guess that Bright Eyes's journey, begun that morning, would lead her some-day to Chicago, New York, and even to the White House in a struggle to save her people.

Bright Eyes grew up during a time of great turmoil for the Omahas. Half the tribe had died in a smallpox epidemic brought by whites at the turn of the century. In 1854, the year Bright Eyes was born, the United States government had forced the Omahas to give up millions of acres of land in exchange for a small area on the Missouri River near present-day Walthill, Nebraska, where they were told they could live in peace.

Moving from the lands of their ancestors caused great sorrow in the tribe but Bright Eyes was too young to notice. She was the second child of two remarkable parents. Both her father, Iron Eye, and her mother, Mary, had Native American mothers and white fathers. Iron Eye's father was a French fur trader who took his son on trapping and hunting expeditions and taught him to speak French. (Iron Eye already spoke a number of tribal languages.) Although Mary and Iron Eye lived according to the native traditions of their mothers, they were also familiar with the white world of their fathers.

When Bright Eyes was a little girl, her parents were still raising their children in the Omaha way. Later, as whites moved into their territory, the family was forced to adapt and change. As she grew up, Bright Eyes was often torn between the two different cultures and traditions.

As soon as Bright Eyes could walk and talk, she learned the rules of Omaha behavior: Never walk between a guest and the fire. Don't stare at strangers. Keep quiet while eating. When sitting, put your legs to one side. Always call your relatives by the name that tells their relationship to you — *Witinu*: Older Brother; *Wihe*: Sister; *Indádi*: Father.

Even as a tiny child, Bright Eyes was given jobs. She gathered firewood and cultivated corn with a hoe made from an elk's shoulder bone. She carried her younger brother, Francis, on his cradle board when he was too young to walk. In her free time, she played *konci*, a game with dice made from plum pits. "Scorched black, [they] had little stars and quarter-moons instead of numbers," she remembered.

In the spring, Bright Eyes accompanied her family on the annual buffalo hunt. She helped the women move the tepees and ponies and listened in awe as her brother Louis described killing his first buffalo. The family "sat around a great fire, roasting the buffalo ribs," Bright Eyes said. "The bit of prairie where the tribe had camped had a clear little stream running through it, with shadowy hills around." Her brothers brought out a drum and "called for a dance." Bright Eyes danced for her family as the flames rose and fell.

When Bright Eyes was seven, Standing Bear, a Ponca chief, visited her family. Bright Eyes stared at the tall, imposing man with piercing black eyes who wore a bear-claw necklace. Bright

*Standing Bear, the Ponca chief who became a nationally known leader and spokesman for Native American causes*

Eyes was too shy to speak to the great chief, but years later, Standing Bear would change her life.

Bright Eyes grew up watching her father struggle to save his people. Iron Eye complained that "white men came, just as the blackbirds do, and spread over the country." White hunters were slaughtering the buffalo. Omahas depended on the buffalo for food. They also used their hides for bedding, their skins for tents, and their bones for tools. How would they live if the buffalo disappeared?

Iron Eye decided that the Omaha could only survive if they became farmers and adopted white ways. He began calling himself Joseph LaFlesche, after his French father, and built the first frame house on Omaha land. When more Omaha families followed his example, Joseph LaFlesche's ideas caused a split in the tribe. Omahas who lived in traditional round earthen lodges and tents mocked the new homes with square corners. They called Joseph's settlement the "Village of the Make-Believe White Men."

Some Omaha men refused to become farmers. Farming was a woman's job! But Joseph was stubborn in his beliefs, too, which also included the idea that Omaha children should be educated in English. The Presbyterian Church built a mission school nearby and Joseph enrolled his oldest son, Louis. When Bright Eyes was eight, her father also took her to the tall, stone building on the hill, a few miles from home.

Bright Eyes's world was now turned upside down. She was torn between the comfortable ways of her Omaha family and the strange customs of white people who called her by her English name, Susette. At first, she was terrified of the school with its three flights of stairs and an attic that Louis told her was haunted by ghosts.

Living at the school on weekdays, Bright Eyes missed her soft deerskin clothes, her thick buffalo-robe bed, and the cozy nights with her grandmother, who still lived in her earthen lodge. She was horrified when teachers cut off the boys' treasured scalp locks, and she hated her baggy "Mother Hubbard" dress. If she spoke Omaha rather than English, her teachers rapped her knuckles with a ruler. Boys were punished even more severely, by being whipped with a hickory stick.

Bright Eyes was miserable at first. But she quickly learned to read and write and fell in love with books and drawing. When she was bored with a lesson, she liked to sketch and doodle on her slate. One teacher, Miss Read, noticed her sketches. Bright Eyes expected to be punished for not paying attention, but Miss Read said that her drawings were *ou-daa* (meaning "good" in Omaha). Bright Eyes began to draw Omaha scenes: a baby on a cradle board, a woman pounding corn, an Omaha warrior, the tent that held the Sacred White Buffalo.

The mission school opened a door into the white world for Bright Eyes, as her father had hoped. But it also brought tragedy to her family. Cooped up in the stuffy dormitory rooms, many children came down with white people's diseases, such as measles, pneumonia, and tuberculosis. One winter morning, Bright Eyes's brother was not at breakfast and no one would tell her where he was. Breaking the rules, she slipped up the stairs to the boys' dormitory and discovered Louis alone, shaking with fever. She sent a message to her family, and a relative raced to the school to bring Louis to the Omaha healer. It was too late; Louis died in a few days. At his funeral, lines of boys and men impaled willow branches into the flesh of their left arms to show their sorrow. Bright Eyes drew the symbol of death: an arrow with an unstrung bow.

Bright Eyes painted the same picture a few years later when she heard that the mission school would shut down. It was 1869

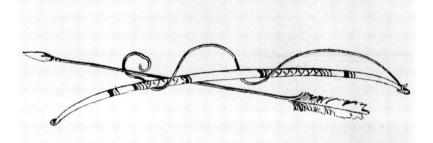

*Bright Eyes often drew this picture of an arrow with an unstrung bow, the Omaha symbol of death or endings. This drawing is from* Ooh-mah-ha Ta-wa-tha, *a book she illustrated about Omaha life and customs.*

and Bright Eyes was fifteen. She went home feeling lost and confused. Was she Bright Eyes, who knew the prayers to the Omaha god, Wakonda? Or Susette, who could sing Presbyterian hymns and was teaching her three younger sisters to speak English?

Bright Eyes stayed home for two years, rereading her few books and longing to return to school. One winter day, she received a letter from Miss Read, her former teacher, now teaching in the East. What would Bright Eyes like for Christmas?

Bright Eyes felt greedy, but she wrote back saying she only wanted one gift: an education. To her surprise, Miss Read replied with good news. Some friends in the East had raised enough money for Bright Eyes to attend a private girls' school in New Jersey. The next fall, Bright Eyes left the open prairies of her childhood for the Elizabeth Institute. In her four years away, she excelled in literature and writing, and was first in her class in every subject but mathematics.

When Bright Eyes came home from New Jersey, the tribe was in deep trouble. The buffalo were disappearing, the wheat crop had failed, and no one could leave the reservation without permission from the government agent. Even worse, Congress had forced the Omahas to share their reservation with the Winnebago Indians. Tribal leaders turned to Bright Eyes right away, asking her to help them write to the federal government about their suffering.

Bright Eyes took down their words. An older Omaha named White Eagle had her write, "When people lose what they hold dear to them, the heart cries all the time."

Bright Eyes was sad, too. She was rereading a book of poetry by George MacDonald, given to her by the school in New Jersey. She had underlined the phrases "Be thou strong" and "Go and do the deed." Bright Eyes was determined to educate Omaha children, so they could grow up to write their own letters. But the agent refused to let her travel to a nearby town to take the teacher's exam. One night, Bright Eyes galloped off on her horse, passed the test, and came back with her certificate.

Next she had to persuade the agent to let her open a school. After many months of begging, he finally gave Bright Eyes a rundown building. There was no money for books, and Bright Eyes was paid half of a normal teaching salary. She struggled to teach eighty Omaha children and a few whites while snow drifted through holes in the roof. Because the buffalo were gone, mothers had no skins to make moccasins for their children. Some students walked the two miles to school barefoot over snow and ice; they left bloody footprints on the schoolroom floor. In spite of the terrible conditions, Bright Eyes's school was a success. She even prepared her younger sisters,

Susan and Marguerite, so well that they also attended her former high school in New Jersey.

One cold March morning in 1879, the Omaha children arrived at school behaving strangely. Bright Eyes guessed they carried a secret they couldn't speak out loud, for fear the white children in the class would hear them. Finally, they whispered the news in Omaha: Chief Standing Bear had arrived in the night, with thirty other starving Poncas. They were all hiding in the village.

Bright Eyes couldn't concentrate. As soon as the day's lessons were done, she hurried home. The once proud, imposing chief she had met as a child was now gaunt and exhausted, his moccasins caked with blood. Bright Eyes and her family listened to Standing Bear's story. A few months earlier, he said, the government had mistakenly given his land to the Sioux and banished all the Poncas to Indian Territory (now Oklahoma). "We had nothing to do there but sit still, be sick, starve, and die," he said. Standing Bear's son was one of hundreds who died. The boy's final request to his parents was to be buried in his homeland. Standing Bear and a small band of followers stole away, carrying the boy's body in a wooden box. They traveled hundreds of miles on foot, through winter storms, to their Omaha friends and relatives.*

The Omahas were horrified by this story. They gave the stranded Poncas food and shelter, but American soldiers soon heard they were hiding in Joseph's village. The soldiers captured the Poncas and locked them up at Fort Omaha, about seventy miles away.

---

* The Ponca, Omaha, Kansa, and Osage people belong to the same language group, and many are also related through marriage.

Stranded inside the fort, Standing Bear and his band were near despair. The government had ordered them to return to Indian Territory. Then Bright Eyes and her family heard amazing news: Thomas H. Tibbles, a fiery editor at the *Omaha Daily Herald*, had taken up the Ponca cause. Tibbles had persuaded Judge Dundy in the town of Omaha to hear the Poncas' case—and had also found two respected lawyers to represent them in court.

Who was this man Tibbles? Bright Eyes wondered. And why was he so eager to save Standing Bear and his band? She wrote a passionate letter to the newspaper, describing the Poncas' hardships and sending along a statement which the Poncas had dictated to her. "I do hope some action will be taken on this matter soon," she wrote. Tibbles was also curious about the eloquent writer, who signed her letter Susette LaFlesche.

Bright Eyes met Tibbles when she and her father arrived in the courtroom to watch the trial. Bright Eyes was impressed by the white newspaper editor with the unruly mop of hair who was determined to save the Poncas. Tibbles saw a small, shy, dark-eyed woman who wore a plain black dress. Soon, their lives would be entwined.

Judge Dundy listened to the government's testimony, which claimed that Indians had no rights because they were not people. Then the Poncas presented their case, including a moving plea from Standing Bear that made many spectators weep. "Two years ago I had a house," Standing Bear said. "I built it with my own hands. . . . I had horses and cattle. Now I have nothing but a tent."

The judge handed down his decision in a few days. "I must hold," he wrote, "that Indians . . . are persons." The Poncas, he said, should never have been moved or held against their will. Standing Bear and his band were set free.

Bright Eyes and her family rejoiced with the Poncas. But where could the Poncas go now? The land of their ancestors was occupied by the Sioux. The government claimed the Poncas were happy in Indian Territory, yet Standing Bear had described the tribe as suffering from hunger and disease. Who was telling the truth? Standing Bear's band asked Bright Eyes and her father to travel to Indian Territory and come back with their findings. Joseph and Bright Eyes were especially worried about their Ponca cousins who had remained in Indian Territory.

Bright Eyes was appalled by what they saw there. When she returned home, a minister asked her to speak to his church members about her trip. Bright Eyes was reluctant at first. Talk in front of a huge crowd? She was much too shy. But then she thought of the suffering Poncas. If she didn't speak for them, who would?

When she climbed into the pulpit, Bright Eyes was so nervous her voice came out in a whisper. But she grew bolder as she went on speaking. "The first objects we saw were the graves," she said; many had been dug by children for their dead parents. The government agent lived in a fancy house while Bright Eyes's relatives, half-starved, shivered in tents. All their horses had died or been stolen by whites, so the Poncas had no way to hunt and they were too weak to raise their own food. One of her cousins looked "as though all hope had gone out of her life."

When she finished speaking, women wept, men shouted, and Thomas Tibbles, seated in the crowd, made a decision. He was already planning to take Standing Bear on a tour of eastern cities, to raise support for the Ponca cause. If Bright Eyes could excite an audience this way, she should come along as Standing Bear's translator.

At first, her father refused to let Bright Eyes go. It wasn't proper for a young Omaha woman to travel with two men! But Joseph changed his mind when Tibbles suggested that they take Bright Eyes's brother Frank along as a chaperone and second interpreter. He also promised Joseph that Bright Eyes could speak for the Omahas, too.

Their first stop was Chicago. Bright Eyes thought she would only act as a translator, but soon she was being interviewed by reporters. "I want to make known the wrongs done to my people," she told them. "Are Indians the only people in this country who have no rights?" When Bright Eyes arrived in Boston, local newspapers had already announced the arrival of "a very interesting young lady, who speaks English fluently."

The group began an exhausting round of speech making. They appeared in churches, theaters, and crowded auditoriums. According to the *Boston Daily Advertiser*, Standing Bear addressed the audience in his official chief's dress "of strong colors, red, green, and gold-work." Bright Eyes wore eastern clothing: "a mantilla coat and black velvet bonnet, neatly trimmed with beads."

Standing Bear spoke first, with Bright Eyes interpreting his pleas for justice. When Bright Eyes gave her own speech, audiences were spellbound. She was the first woman of any race to speak in Boston's Faneuil Hall, the birthplace of the American Revolution. The galleries were full and people stood in the aisles as she cried, "We are thinking men and women who have souls to be saved! We want to be able to call our lands our own."

Bright Eyes was becoming a bold speaker. "When the Indian . . . fights for his property, liberty, and life," she said, "they call him a savage. When the first settlers fought for their property, liberty, and lives, they were called heroes." Wherever she spoke, audiences

*Bright Eyes (Susette LaFlesche) in eastern dress, about 1890*

passed resolutions, raised money, and wrote to newspapers, Congress, and the president. The group traveled to Philadelphia, then Washington, D.C., where Bright Eyes met President and Mrs. Hayes and testified before Congress.

Bright Eyes had left her village a shy, unknown Omaha woman. She came home a national celebrity who had shared the stage with famous Americans, from state officials to abolitionists who had worked to stop slavery, to writers and artists—even the celebrated poet Henry Wadsworth Longfellow. "If I could speak before them," she boasted, "I could speak before anybody."

In 1881, Bright Eyes married Thomas Tibbles, whose wife had died, and took on the care of his two daughters. After her marriage, Bright Eyes continued to write and speak on behalf of her people. She toured the United States a number of times and traveled to England. Bright Eyes also achieved success as a writer. She published regular essays in the *Weekly Independent* in Nebraska and edited books by other Native American leaders. A story called "Nedawi," based on her childhood, was published in the children's magazine *St. Nicholas,* the first story published in English by a Native American woman. She also returned to her love of art, illustrating a book about Omaha life.

In spite of her success in the white world, Bright Eyes always missed her family and felt confused about where she belonged. After living in Lincoln, Nebraska, for many years, she and Tibbles returned to the reservation, but her life there was also difficult. Some of her relatives blamed Tibbles for the unfair way the government had divided up their land, and Bright Eyes was never able to mend this rift in her family.

She was also changing her mind about many of her father's ideas. It was wrong, she thought now, to send Omaha children off to school in the East. She believed that the Omaha should become citizens—but that they shouldn't have to give up their language, religion, or way of life in order to become free Americans.

Once, the Omaha shared huge tracts of land; now, they fought over small parcels. Once, they worshipped their god, Wakonda; now, elders no longer taught religious ceremonies to the young.

*Bright Eyes in her Lincoln, Nebraska, home, surrounded by
Omaha weaving and artifacts*

Joseph LaFlesche himself had given away some of the tribe's
most sacred objects. When he died soon afterward, many Omahas believed he was struck down in punishment for his actions.

Sitting Bull, the great chief of the Sioux, once predicted that
if Native Americans were educated by whites, they would end
up neither white nor Indian. Perhaps this had happened to
Bright Eyes. She couldn't heal the split that opened inside herself when she first left her parents' house to attend the mission
school and became known as Susette. But she had helped to
launch the Indian rights movement and had awakened many
Americans to the suffering and injustices inflicted on native
people all over the country.

Bright Eyes's house on her Omaha land. Bright Eyes is in
the upstairs window; her husband, Thomas Tibbles, and his
daughters are seated outside.

While Bright Eyes had returned to the reservation to live, her
younger sister Susan—who had learned to read and write in
Bright Eyes's school—was following her own very different path as
she struggled to improve the health of the Omaha people.

THE STUFFY BEDROOM smelled of medicine and oint-ment. Susan LaFlesche sat quietly by the sickbed, her dark eyes watching her patient while her half-brother Francis and his friends chanted a healing song. The men sang softly, without their drums. They didn't want to upset the patient, a famous anthropologist named Alice Fletcher. Fletcher had become very sick while she was studying the Omaha way of life.

Susan LaFlesche was eighteen in the summer of 1883 when she offered to help with Miss Fletcher's care. While she bathed the older woman and gave her medicine for her pain, argu-ments about the best way to treat her patient buzzed outside the sickroom like angry hornets. Some elders insisted they shouldn't rely on the government doctor. Wasn't it his fault that Fletcher had lost her thick chestnut hair? Others claimed Fletcher was being punished for trying to steal their tribal secrets. Some, like

Francis, believed that singing or tribal remedies would help her.

If only Susan could cure Miss Fletcher! Like her older sister Bright Eyes, Susan had gone to high school in New Jersey, but her study of the "common branches"—arithmetic, literature, and philosophy—hadn't prepared her for nursing. Instead, she was an assistant teacher at the reservation school. She didn't fit in there and she felt stifled in her father's tiny frame house crowded with relatives. And although she was an excellent rider and had been doing farm chores since she was a little girl, Susan didn't want to settle down and raise cattle like others in her family. "You won't catch me anywhere near the cows," she announced to her sister Rosalie.

As Miss Fletcher slowly recovered, Susan talked with the older woman, sharing her worries about the tribe's health. Many Omahas suffered from white men's diseases they couldn't prevent or cure. Once, her people lived in spacious earthen lodges, big enough for three families. Now, families were shut up in stuffy rooms where illness spread easily. For years, the Omaha had hunted buffalo, eating their dried meat through the winter. But the buffalo hunts ended when Susan was eight, after eastern white hunters slaughtered the great herds. Now, Omahas who couldn't raise their own cattle ate government beef, which often spoiled and made them sick.

During her talks with Miss Fletcher, a secret dream began to grow inside Susan. Miss Fletcher later remembered that Susan told her "how she desired to study medicine, that she might instruct her Indian friends in . . . health and minister to them in sickness."

Alice Fletcher recognized that Susan had special talent. "I determined as I saw her mental ability that she should have her

*Susan LaFlesche (seated on right) and her sister Marguerite at the Elizabeth Institute in Elizabeth, New Jersey, the school they attended as teenagers*

wish," Fletcher wrote. Within a year, Miss Fletcher had raised enough money to send both Susan and her sister Marguerite to the Hampton Institute in Virginia.

At first, Susan's parents, as well as her grandmother, Nicomi, didn't want the girls to go. The Hampton Institute, a school for freed slaves and Native Americans, was coeducational, and at that time, Omaha boys and girls—even young women Susan's age—didn't date or spend time together unless they were chaperoned. But Fletcher and other easterners convinced Susan's parents that Hampton watched its students carefully.

So the two sisters loosened their dark braids, pulled their hair back with ribbons, and dressed in heavy, dark skirts and blouses. They left their ponies behind, said good-bye to the family, and boarded the eastbound train.

In her first weeks at Hampton, Susan made friends quickly. Although she never felt as pretty as Marguerite, she was outgoing, active, and fun loving. Soon, she was meeting Native American boys, including a boy named Ashley who walked her home after church. "The girls tease me unmercifully about Ashley," she wrote to her sister Rosalie. "You can't imagine."

But a shy young Sioux named Tom Ikinicapi (whom she called T.I.) stole Susan's heart. T.I. only spoke a little English and was having trouble in his classes. Susan admired his determination to learn and his quiet loyalty to her. She said he was "*without exception* the handsomest Indian I ever saw."

Unlike Marguerite, who was thrilled to have a boyfriend and planned to marry him when they graduated, Susan was torn apart by her feelings. If she married T.I., would she have to give up her dream of serving her people? Like many other women of her time, she knew it would be difficult to have a career and raise a family. In one sad letter to Rosalie she said, "Nothing will come of it."

While she struggled with these feelings, Susan studied hard and developed skills in drawing and music. She also found time to work as a volunteer, reading to older black women in the community. Her fine record at the Hampton Institute made her family proud. She graduated second in her class and gave the salutatorian's speech, titled "My Girlhood and Womanhood." In her speech Susan said, "Some people have to wait for their work to be revealed to them, but from the outset, the work of an Indian girl is plain before her."

Susan received two surprises at graduation. She learned that she had been accepted to study at the Women's Medical College of Philadelphia. And she earned a gold medal for receiving the highest marks on her final exam. According to a local paper, the audience—which included Alice Fletcher—greeted her with "thunderous applause" when she received her medal.

Susan left Hampton with mixed feelings. It hurt to say goodbye to T.I., who needed one more year to graduate. "Perhaps he won't come back, or he may come back . . . married," Susan wrote to Rosalie. "But I am sure that wouldn't break my heart for 'I ain't made that way.' " Still, she admitted, "I should like to see him again."

In spite of missing T.I., Susan described her last vacation at home, before medical school, as a "happy, golden summer." Although the Hampton Institute had given her a good education, the school's mission was to make its Native American and African American students become more like whites. In Nebraska, Susan could be herself—a young Omaha woman. When fall came, it was hard for Susan to board the train. No

Native American woman had ever tried to become a doctor. Could she succeed? So many people were relying on her. The Connecticut Indian Association, a group that helped Native Americans around the country, had raised all the money for her tuition, travel, and living expenses. She couldn't let them down.

The day Susan registered at the Women's Medical College of Philadelphia, the dean rose from her chair and kissed her. "We welcome you and are proud of your lineage," the dean said. The dean had learned about Susan's achievements from the head of the Hampton Institute, and she also knew about Susan's famous older sister, Bright Eyes.

No one in Philadelphia realized how hard Susan had struggled to gain her education. Nor could they guess about the life she'd left behind. Dressed in blue flannel with her hair piled high in the latest style, Susan seemed at ease with eastern ways. Yet everything about city life was different from the reservation. Instead of sleeping on a buffalo robe in a room with her sisters, Susan had her own room, which she decorated with Christmas cards, photographs, and pictures. In the Omaha village, Susan had drawn water from the well and helped her mother and her father's second wife with the cooking. (Omaha chiefs often had two, or even three, wives.) When the meal was served, everyone—including Susan's grandmother, Nicomi—sat on the floor to eat, and no one took a bite until her father, Joseph, prayed to their god, Wakonda.

In Philadelphia, Susan sat around a table with other women, and she never had to worry, as she had at home, about whether she would have enough food. If she wanted to visit with a friend, she didn't jump on her pony and gallop down a dusty road. Instead, she cranked the telephone box on the wall or climbed on a trolley.

*Susan LaFlesche, in a photograph taken after she returned to Nebraska as a physician*

As Susan struggled to adapt to all these changes, she fell in love with medical school. "It is splendid," she wrote Rosalie in her weekly letter home. She studied anatomy, chemistry, and physiology and never skipped a class, because she had to make a grade of 90 on every test to pass. She visited the museum, where she was thrilled to learn that each part of a bone had a name. And she looked forward to her first dissection. "I am going to wield the knife tonight," she wrote. The body was divided into six areas, and two students dissected each part. "We take off little by little," Susan wrote her sister, "first the skin, then the tissue, then some muscle is lifted, showing arteries, veins, nerves, etc." Susan was never squeamish. "We laugh and talk . . . just as we do anywhere," she said.

Susan was also excited to observe her first operation in a Philadelphia hospital. As she filed into the cold operating room with the other students, the famous surgeon Dr. Keen singled her out. "You are the first woman of your tribe . . . to go back and practice among your people," he said. She never took her eyes off Dr. Keen as he picked up his scalpel and prepared to cut a tumor from a child's back.

Suddenly, there was a commotion on the other side of the room. One of the men from Jefferson Medical College, who was also observing the surgery, had fainted dead away. His fellow students carried him quickly into the hall.

Susan never flinched. "None of the girls were *thinking* of fainting," she wrote to Rosalie afterward. "I think no more of seeing an amputation now . . . than I do to see a patient who has fever."

As she inched toward becoming a full-fledged doctor, Susan's heart still ached for T.I. She spent her winter vacation at Hampton and was surprised to discover that T.I. continued to care for her. "I'm afraid it is Deep Waters with him," she admitted to Rosalie. But she had promised the women of the Connecticut Indian Association that she would practice medicine for a few years before she married. In the end, she had to tell T.I. that they could never be together. "I shall be the dear little old maid," she wrote to Rosalie.

Susan studied hard, but she also found time to play. After exams, the students celebrated with a taffy pull. On weekends,

Susan was invited to the homes of fellow students, including one elegant mansion where the coffee was served "in a great big silver urn with a flame under it." She went to the Academy of Fine Arts, attended musicals such as *The Mikado*, and visited Independence Hall when her brother Frank came to town. Unfortunately, they had to leave the historic spot because too many tourists were staring at *them*, rather than the Liberty Bell.

Susan had no extra spending money, but her life was still much easier than it had been on the reservation. When an older friend gave Susan a dollar to buy herself a pair of fashionable kid gloves, Susan sent the money to her family instead. Her mother was sick, and Susan wanted Rosalie to buy her some meat. "I am going to send besides a little packet of Carbolated Vaseline and Castile soap," Susan wrote. "Of course [Mother] knows I would gladly give my life for her."

Except for a friend who was teaching at the nearby Lincoln School for Native Americans, no one in Philadelphia realized how much Susan missed her family. Only her letters to her sister Rosalie told the truth. "What is the riches and knowledge that can compare to my own dear family?" Susan asked.

She also longed for the freedom of the open prairie. "Dear me, what a wild, harum-scarum thing I used to be," she wrote to Rosalie. "I can't cut up here or sing or dance for the children. . . . I don't want to grow old and quiet before my time." Still, Susan made her own outdoor fun, walking in snowy Fairmont Park with a friend, drying her feet in the oven afterward, and strumming her friend's guitar while singing songs she had learned at Hampton.

Susan felt most alone when her relatives were sick. In her last year of school, Rosalie sent her a telegram: Their father was very ill. Susan borrowed money and took the first train home, but she was too late. Joseph had already died. She nearly quit school, until Rosalie reminded her how their father had counted on his children being educated. After the funeral, Susan forced herself to return to Philadelphia and her studies.

As she prepared to practice medicine on the reservation, Susan began doctoring her family in her letters. "I think Mother doesn't have the right food or her foot would be better," she wrote. She sent Rosalie a long list of suggestions for improving her health. For Rosalie's husband, Susan said, "Tell Ed, Doctor Sue prescribes less quinine and more time for his meals."

After three years at the Women's Medical College, Susan returned to Nebraska as the first Native American woman to earn a medical degree. Although she graduated first in her class and had also interned at a fine Philadelphia hospital after graduation, the government agent refused to hire her as the reservation doctor. Instead, he put her to work at the school at a very low salary.

Susan was disappointed at first, but she soon realized that treating sick children gave her a chance to doctor their families, too. She talked to parents about cleanliness and healthy food, and taught them that germs could spread when children went to school with a bad cold, or drank from the same cup. She urged the government to send enough money for vision and dental care as well as medicines. "I shall fight good and hard against anything that is to the tribe's detriment, even if I have to fight alone," she wrote.

After a few years, she was finally hired as the reservation doctor. She traveled long distances on horseback or in a covered carriage to see patients. Because there were few nurses and no local hospital, Susan often had to stay with her patients until they improved. When her nephew Eddie had the flu, Susan spent three

*Dr. Susan LaFlesche (second from the left, holding a baby)
attending a meeting of the Native American Church on
the Omaha reservation*

days at his bedside, feeding him ice and watching over him until
he was well. When she was at home, Susan kept a lantern lit in
her window all night to help patients find their way to her door.

In spite of her long hours and the endless miles she covered visiting patients on isolated farms, Susan received the same salary as
when she had been the school doctor. Her sisters were outraged,
but Susan didn't complain. She had finally achieved her dream.

Although Susan had predicted she would die an "old maid," she married Henry Picotte when she was twenty-nine. Henry was an Omaha friend who had returned to the reservation after being a circus performer. The Picottes had two sons and settled in the new town of Walthill, where Susan proved that a woman could have a career *and* a family.

As Susan traveled about the reservation treating the sick, she realized how some government policies had created bad health for the tribe. Like Bright Eyes, she began to think that adapting to the white world had caused serious problems for the Omaha. She tried to learn more about Omaha religious ceremonies and began to speak out about the tribe's needs.

Now that the Omahas no longer had chiefs, many members turned to Susan as their leader. Susan had never planned to take on a public role, as Bright Eyes did, but when the tribe had a dispute with the government over their lands, they insisted that Susan go to Washington to meet with the Office of Indian Affairs. "It makes me feel so good to know all the Omahas had such confidence in me," she said.

Susan grew disappointed with the Connecticut Indian Association, which had sent her to medical school. Its members never lived up to their promise to help her establish a hospital on the reservation. Susan raised the money herself and eventually built a hospital in Walthill, the first to care for Omahas and whites side by side.

In later years, friends boasted that Susan had treated every Omaha at least once. She also cared for her mother, Mary, and her sister Bright Eyes in their final days. As she had predicted to Rosalie long ago, she had "come home to doctor and dose you all."

*The hospital that Dr. Susan LaFlesche built in Walthill, Nebraska,
the first to treat Caucasians and Native Americans side by side*

---

While the wide expanses of prairie land filled with settlers, California continued to draw adventurous people from all over the world, including thousands of Chinese who crossed the Pacific Ocean seeking the land they called "Gold Mountain."

> *"Is it a Disgrace to be born a Chinese? Didn't God make us All!!!"*
>
> **Mary McGladery Tape**
>
> ———◆◆◆———
>
> 1857–1928

A SMALL CHILD LEANED against the rail, her dark eyes watching as the port of Shanghai disappeared for-ever. Gulls wheeled and screeched over the ship. The little girl was leaving China for *Gum San*, or Gold Mountain—the Chinese name for California.

The child was only eleven when she embarked on her adven-ture. "I was born in the northern part of China, near Shanghai," she remembered. Few people from her area had ever immigrated to America. She had been orphaned when she was young and raised by Presbyterian missionaries in Shanghai. They gave her a Scottish name: Mary McGladery.

We don't know why the missionaries decided to bring Mary to California. She probably had no choice in the matter. In Mary's time, some girls who were born into China's terrible poverty were brought to America as prostitutes and forced to live in tiny "cribs" no bigger than a jail cell. Others became *mui jai* (servant girls) who stayed with their employers until they were grown. In wealthier Chinese families, the parents bound their daughters' feet in a painful process which forced them to walk in tiny, mincing steps and kept them close to home. But Mary would never be owned by anyone—and she could run freely up and down the ship's deck because her feet had never been bound.

Mary was following thousands of Chinese men who had left home to seek their fortunes. They were fleeing the wars, poverty, and famine that raged throughout China in the nineteenth century. Ever since gold had been discovered in 1848, Chinese men had traveled to *Gum San* by sea, but most left their wives, daughters, and sisters behind. Mary was one of the few Chinese girls or women who immigrated to California at that time.

In 1868, the year Mary crossed the Pacific, boat travel was cramped and difficult. We don't know if Mary rode on a sailing vessel or a steamer, since steamships had only been introduced the year before. On many boats, hundreds of Chinese men were crammed below the decks on bunks stacked up like playing cards. The stuffy air in the hold smelled like vomit and sweat. The food was terrible, and many Chinese were afraid to eat meals prepared by the *fan qui* (foreign devils) who operated the ships. There was never enough fresh water on any boat, so Mary and her fellow travelers couldn't take baths or wash their clothes.

Storms and rough seas made everyone seasick, and disease swept through the hold. On some ships, one of every ten passengers died. It took six to eight weeks for most sailing vessels to reach San Francisco.

By the time Mary arrived, the gold rush was slowing down. In the twenty years since the first gold nugget had been found, San Francisco had become a bustling city known to the Chinese as *Dai Fou*, or Big City. It was now connected to the rest of the country by telegraph lines, and the transcontinental railroad was nearly finished. Within a year, trains would replace covered wagons, making it easier for travelers to cross the country in both directions.

No one knows whether Mary was met at the dock, or how she found her way to the missionary school. Years after her arrival, Mary told her story to a reporter from a San Francisco newspaper. "I have not much recollection of the first few months of my time here," she said, "except that I spent some time in Chinatown."

At that time, Chinatown was already a lively corner of the city, packed into six short blocks. Butcher shops, boardinghouses, tailors, and Chinese groceries were tucked tight against each other. Chinese men with long queues (braids) hurried up the steep streets, carrying fresh produce over their shoulders in double-ended bamboo baskets. Restaurants competed to see which could come up with the most poetic sign. One called itself a "fragrant almond chamber," while another boasted it had "customers coming like clouds."

Walking through Chinatown, the smells of sandalwood, incense, smoky tea, and roast pork must have made Mary feel as if she were back in China. Wind chimes jingled from balconies and colored paper lanterns swung in the breeze. There was even a Chinese opera house which produced Chinese plays and music. And on the Chinese New Year, residents came from all over the city to watch the fireworks, which were set off to scare away evil spirits.

*San Francisco's Chinatown in the 1860s, about the time of*
*Mary McGladery's arrival*

After five months in Chinatown, Mary said she was "taken up by the Ladies Relief Society on Franklin Street." The society was run by Presbyterian missionaries. "It was under their care," Mary remembered, "that I first learned to speak the English language and acquire American manners." The education Mary received changed her life. Having an education was very unusual for a Chinese girl of her time. In the 1860s and 1870s, only twenty percent of Chinese children in California went to school—and most students were boys.

Mary stayed with the missionaries for five years. Soon after she left, she met Joseph Tape, a young man who had also come to California as a child and received his education through the Presbyterian church. He had worked hard since he was a young boy. At first, he delivered milk on horseback for a man who ran a dairy ranch. Later, he moved freight for an express company and worked as a translator for the Chinese consulate. "We were married after a six month courtship," Mary remembered.

Mary had survived all these years without parents or brothers and sisters. Now she could start a family of her own. A year after their marriage, the Tape's first child, Mamie, was born; eventually, they also had a son, Frank, and two more daughters.

It was not easy for a Chinese couple to raise a family in America. Anti-Chinese feeling had been growing steadily worse since Mary had arrived. Californians relied on Chinese workers to clear their swamps for cropland, to grow and pick their produce, and to build their railroads, but they treated them with violence and scorn. One Chinese man remembered, "When I first came, Chinese [were] treated worse than dogs. Oh, it was terrible, terrible. . . . The hoodlums . . . pull your queue, slap your face, throw all kinds of old vegetables and rotten eggs at you."

*A group of Chinese girls from a San Francisco mission. Although
no photographs of Mary exist from this period, she probably wore a
similar uniform when she lived at the Ladies Relief Society.*

By the time Mary's first daughter was born, the economy was
in trouble and Californians were afraid the Chinese would steal
their jobs. In 1877, a mob burned and looted Chinatown for three
days. The Chinese begged the city for protection, but the police
ignored them. The Workingman's Party had a new slogan: "The
Chinese Must Go!" One newspaper announced, "[The Chinese]
are not of our people and never will be." In 1882, Congress passed

the Chinese Exclusion Act, a law that kept most Chinese emigrants from entering the United States until well into the twentieth century. For the first time in history, America had slammed its doors on people of one specific race and culture.

Californians also refused to allow Chinese children into their public schools. For a while, the city ran a separate school for Chinese students in the evenings, so that adults could learn English alongside their children. The school was outside Chinatown, and Chinese children were afraid of being stoned if they attended, so only a few came. From 1871 until 1884, there were no public schools of any kind for the Chinese.

When Mamie Tape was old enough to go to school, San Francisco's superintendent told his principals he would fire anyone who allowed Chinese children into the classroom. But he wasn't prepared for parents like Mary and Joseph Tape. The Tapes believed in the value of education—and in their children's rights as American citizens. "We have always lived as Americans and our children have been brought up as such," Mary said. The Tape children spoke perfect English, wore western-style clothes, attended Presbyterian church, and had many white playmates in their neighborhood. Joseph had even cut off his long queue—a symbol of Chinese citizenship—to show his loyalty to America.

The Tapes wanted Mamie to attend the neighborhood school with her friends, instead of a private Chinese school. After all, they paid taxes, just like their neighbors. Shouldn't they have the same rights?

The school board didn't agree. When Mary and Joseph Tape took Mamie to the Spring Valley School on opening day, the principal turned them away.

Mary Tape was outraged. A recent court case had declared

that children born in the United States were citizens, even if their parents were not. "What right!" Mary wrote to the school board, "have you to bar my child out of the school because she is a Chinese?"

Perhaps Mary remembered that when she was Mamie's age, she had no parents to stand up for her. Perhaps she thought of the women at the Ladies Relief Society, whose precious gift of an education had provided her with opportunities few Chinese girls ever had, whether they lived in China or California. When the superintendent refused to let Mamie into school, Mary and Joseph took the city to court.

At first, the Tapes were successful. The judge ruled that the parents' "application to the Spring Valley School is lawful and must be granted." When the city appealed the case to the State Supreme Court, those judges also sided with the Tapes. Because Mamie was a citizen, they said she had the "same right to enter a public school as any other child."

The Tapes and their lawyers showed up at the school again, but the principal still turned Mamie away, saying she didn't have the proper vaccination letter from a doctor. In fact, the principal was just stalling. He knew that the state legislature had planned an emergency session. As expected, they passed a new law allowing the city to set up separate public schools for Chinese children.

In April of 1885, five months after Mary and Joseph Tape had started their battle with the school board, Mamie was still at home. Her mother wrote a bold, angry letter to the Board of Education. The letter appeared on the front page of the *Alta California*, one of San Francisco's daily newspapers. "Dear Sirs," Mary wrote, "I see that you are going to make all sorts of excuses to keep my child out of the public schools. Dear sirs, will you please tell me! Is it a disgrace to be born a Chinese? Didn't God make us all!!!"

She went on to say that she hoped the superintendent would never be persecuted as her daughter had been. "Mamie Tape will never attend any of the Chinese schools of your making! Never!!!"

But Mary's passionate pleas couldn't move the school board or the superintendent. Mary Tape and her husband had won the right for a public education, but it was only a partial victory. Their children still couldn't attend school in their own neighborhood. In the end, Mamie Tape and her brother—and later, their two younger sisters—went to a new public school for Chinese children in Chinatown.

Mary Tape was certainly discouraged by these events. But while she was making news for her fight against discrimination, Mary was also becoming known for her achievements in photography and science—two unusual pursuits for women of her time. A few years after her battle with the school board, a newspaper article appeared describing Mary's work with a scientist named Tong Hai Wong, an inventor experimenting with new technology.

At the end of the nineteenth century, the telephone, the telegraph, and advances in photography were changing the way Americans communicated with each other. Private telephones were rare, yet Mr. Wong and the Tapes, along with fourteen other families, had connected telephone and telegraph lines between their houses over a distance of six miles. Mary and her husband were both experts in Morse code, the special signals used to communicate by telegraph. The telegraphic device for sending and receiving messages sat on the Tape's dining-room table. This allowed Mary to "talk" with Joseph at his business.

*Mary and Joseph Tape and their four grown children. Standing (left to right): Gertrude, Frank, and Emily. Seated: Mary, Mamie (the subject of the court case), and Joseph*

The clicking of dots and dashes, which she could hear from all over the house, also told her if Mr. Wong wanted to "discuss science at long range." Thanks to a series of sliding switches in her home, she and Mr. Wong could speak on the telephone, too. Mary Tape was breaking the rules of her time. At the turn of the century, it was rare for a woman to know as much about new technology as Mary did.

*Joseph and Mary Tape near the end of their long life together.*
*Sadly, none of the photographs Mary took survive.*

Mary was even more dedicated to her experiments in photography. When photography was first invented, photographers coated plates of glass with a special wet solution and had to develop the plates immediately. For this reason, they hauled their darkrooms with them whenever they wanted to take a picture. The equipment was too heavy and cumbersome for most women to carry, so only a few were able to become photographers in the early days. When smaller cameras and dry plates were invented, it was easier for both women and men to take pictures in the field and then bring the plates back to their darkrooms for developing. Mary, who had a darkroom in her house, was among the first women to take advantage of these new techniques.

"I not only take my own pictures but prepare my own plates and make my own prints," Mary said. When asked how she learned about the business, Mary answered, "Everything I know has come from reading different authorities on the subjects and then studying the methods to see which was best." Every summer, Mary's family traveled to different parts of the state and Mary brought home new landscapes and portraits. "I always make a success of the majority of my pictures," Mary said proudly.

Mary and Mr. Wong were also working on a camera that had a faster shutter speed. This meant her subjects didn't have to hold still quite as long. Mary wanted to aim her camera at horses and birds, to photograph "trotters in motion and birds in their flight." Mary Tape's photographs were printed in San Francisco's *Morning Call* and won awards from the Mechanics Institute. A reporter who studied her work observed that Mary Tape's photos were "far beyond the usual work of amateurs in any country."

Mary Tape's achievements in science and art were unusual for

*An oil painting of chrysanthemums by Mary Tape.*
*Mary's descendants on the West Coast also treasure*
*her painted china plates.*

her time. She was particularly different from most Chinese women of that period. She had been born in a culture that severely restricted women. Chinese men treated women as property and expected them to follow the "three obediences": As a child, a girl obeyed her father; as a young wife, she obeyed her husband; and as an old woman, her son.

Mary was lucky to find a husband who treated her as an equal. As she said later, "We have never had cause to regret our first meeting. . . . Our lives have been very happy." When the Tapes were interviewed by a newspaper reporter in 1892, Joseph expressed his pride in Mary's musical abilities. Thanks to her musical training at the Ladies Relief Society, she was able to teach the three oldest children to play the piano, the French horn, and the violin.

In the same interview, Joseph boasted about his wife's achievements, pointing out Mary's elegant landscape paintings and photographs hanging on the walls, as well as her hand-painted china plates and mirrors decorating their home. According to the reporter, Mary had also "produced still-life paintings of fruit which made [his] mouth water."

In spite of the barriers she faced in California, Mary's education and talents allowed her to take advantage of the opportunities that opened up for women in the American West. Just as her feet had never been bound, her character had also remained unfettered. She had developed the courage to take on battles that other women—as well as men—shied away from. When asked if she and Joseph would ever go back to China, Mary said they would only travel there as tourists. She said, "California is our home. All of our best and happiest moments have been passed here, and here we shall live and die."

◄••►

*For most westerners, the gold rush was now a distant memory. But there was one last discovery to come, which caused a final stampede to the most rugged wilderness of all: the Klondike.*

> *"I wasn't built for going backwards. When I once step forward, I must go ahead."*
>
> **Katherine Ryan: "Klondike Kate"**
>
> ---
>
> **AUGUST 1869–FEBRUARY 1932**

"GOLD! THEY'VE FOUND GOLD!" The paperboy waved a copy of the *Vancouver Sun.* "Gold in the Yukon!"

It was a hot morning in July, 1898. Kate Ryan, a twenty-eight-year-old nurse, was on her way to the hospital in Vancouver, Canada. She hurried to join the crowd around the newsboy. According to the story, a Tagish Indian named Skookum Jim was guzzling water from his hat when he looked down and discovered chunks of gold as "big as beans" floating inside. Skookum Jim and his partners quickly grabbed a frying pan and began finding "nuggets everywhere."

This news was almost a year old when it reached Kate Ryan. Rabbit Creek, where the gold was discovered, was a tributary of the Klondike River. It flowed through a remote region of northern Canada, far from telegraph lines. Once ice locked up the rivers, boat travel stopped and letters took months to reach the outside world. Now that word of the discovery was finally out, it spread up and down the coast like a raging brushfire.

In Seattle, Washington, five thousand people who had heard the news waited for the steamer *Portland* to pull into the harbor. A rough band of miners straggled down the gangway, their suitcases, boxes, and trunks laden with gold weighing more than a ton. One passenger, Ethel Berry, had left California with sixty dollars in her pocket. Now she stood on the deck in a torn dress, waiting for help with her bedroll, which was too heavy to lift alone. It held $100,000 in gold.

Newspaper reporters rushed to interview Berry. What would she tell other women who wanted to go north?

"Why, to stay away, of course," she said.

If Kate Ryan knew about Ethel Berry's advice, she ignored it. Kate had grown up in the wilderness of Johnville, New Brunswick, and she didn't like city life. Besides, times were hard all over the country, and she was restless in her job. Always eager for adventure, Kate said later she was lured by "the call of the wild. That, and nothing else." And so, she said, "I joined the procession."

Her friends were appalled. Had she lost her mind? Women shouldn't travel alone to that part of the world—and how would she get there? Boats could only navigate the Yukon River in summer, and there were no roads or trains. Other warnings appeared in the papers. A woman reporter for the *Skaguay News* warned that "delicate women have no right attempting the trip. . . . Those who love luxury, comfort, and ease would better remain at home. It takes strong, healthy, courageous women to stand the terrible hardships."

At six feet tall, Kate Ryan *was* strong and healthy. As a teenager, she had developed perfect posture by walking on the roof beams of her family's barn. And she had never known much comfort. Her parents, Patrick and Ellen Ryan, had migrated to Canada to escape Ireland's potato famine and had cleared land in the thick forest of New Brunswick. They struggled to feed their family of seven children on the small earnings from their farm and a shop attached to their house. Kate, the youngest, had worked hard since she was little, picking potatoes until her hands were raw, chopping wood, helping her father mind the store and the animals.

Now a fortune beckoned from rivers whose veins of gold, some said, lay as thick as cheese in a sandwich. Kate just needed to figure out which route to take.

There were two ways to reach the remote Klondike. The coastal route, which took passengers up the Yukon River, was only passable in the summer and was very expensive. Kate chose the cheaper, but more dangerous, "All Canada Route," crossing the Alaskan panhandle into Canada. Most of the trip was overland, which was fine with Kate—boats made her seasick.

After a few months, Kate had saved enough money to buy her ticket and supplies. The Canadian government had passed a law requiring Klondike adventurers to bring enough food, tools, and warm clothes to last a year. The *Skaguay News* published a recommended clothing list for women which advised them to avoid their usual tight corsets. Instead, they should bring practical items such as tall "bicycle shoes" (lace-up boots) and a mattress ticking which could be "filled with dried moss."

*Kate Ryan's travels took her from Vancouver, British Columbia,
to the wilds of the Yukon.*

Kate brought her list to the Hudson Bay Company, where a clerk helped her pick out warm clothes, as well as a Winchester rifle, a heavy waterproof mackinaw, a sleeping bag, and an ax. The clerk presented her with a gift: a small black leather bag with a secret pocket. "Any lady with the courage to head out to the Yukon on her own deserves the support of the Hudson Bay Company," he told her.

Kate's food supplies were enormous. She bought fifty pounds of flour, one hundred and fifty pounds each of bacon and split peas, as well as canned milk and fruit. Finally, she purchased her ticket for the steamer *Tees*, scheduled to leave in February. The boat would only take her as far as Wrangell Island, Alaska. How would she get from there to the northern goldfields?

She first thought of pack horses. Kate had ridden horses since she was young, and her father had taught her how to pick out a good animal. But she couldn't find horses sturdy enough to carry heavy loads through deep snow. So Kate spent $100 on a team of huskies and a sled—even though she knew nothing about driving a dog team.

At last, on February 28, 1898, Kate climbed on board the *Tees*. In addition to her dogs, sled, and other equipment, she carried her Bible, a rosary, and a five-dollar gold piece from her friends in Vancouver. They wanted her to invest it for them in the Klondike. When Kate waved good-bye to her friends at the dock, she didn't know if she'd ever see them again. Kate was setting off for one of the most remote stretches of wilderness left on the continent.

Rough seas battered the *Tees* as she headed north with a cargo of men, a few women, and many animals. The horses, sled dogs, cows, chickens, and even a few goats made for a noisy, smelly ride. The steamer passed boats full of disappointed gold seekers

*Miners and their luggage on a beach. Kate Ryan faced*
*similar confusion when she took her gear off the boat on*
*Wrangell Island, Alaska.*

headed south, warning of the dangers ahead. But Kate was too
seasick to notice.

After four days at sea, the ship dumped its passengers and their
cargo on the muddy beach at Wrangell Island. Kate gathered her
supplies, untangled her dogs, and hurried to find a ride to the
mainland. She needed to mush her team up the frozen Stikine
River before the spring thaw melted the ice.

While on the island, Kate visited a troop of Northwest Mounted
Police, who were waiting for a ferry. A friendly Mountie named

George Chalmers offered her a cup of bitter coffee and told her his sad story. The camp's cook had left, and Chalmers had been ordered to take his place. The Mounties were complaining about his terrible meals. Could Kate advise him on cooking dinner?

Fortunately, Kate had grown up in a big family and knew how to cook for a crowd. They set up the stove, then fried pork and baked biscuits. The Mounties wolfed down the food. When their chief officer, Inspector Primrose, praised her cooking, Kate made him an offer: She would cook for his unit until they reached the Canadian border if he would put her name on his list of ferry passengers.

Primrose agreed immediately. The next morning, Kate visited Wrangell's baker. He gave Kate a fistful of sourdough "starter" and taught her how to turn the mix of flour and water into bread, biscuits, and pancakes. Kate didn't realize how much this gift would help her as she began her adventures in the North.

When Kate and the Mounties finally crossed to the mainland, Kate loaded her sled, hitched up her huskies, and buttoned her mackinaw. Kate and her dogs floundered through deep snow and slush as they followed the Mounties up the Stikine River to the town of Dewdney, where it began to rain. Water poured through Kate's tent, soaking her clothes and supplies. The Mounties set up a permanent camp to patrol the border and urged Kate to stay. She had become their friend as well as their cook. But Kate had to push on before the ice melted. Besides, she told a reporter years later, "I wasn't built for going backwards. When I once step forward, I must go ahead." Kate continued north alone.

The Stikine River cut through deep canyons, with rocky walls rising steeply on each side. It was almost unheard of for a woman to travel this route, known as the most treacherous path to the

Klondike. Yet it could be done. One brave African American woman named Lucille Hunter had made the journey with her husband the year before—while she was nine months pregnant!

Trudging behind her dogs, Kate traveled eight to ten grueling miles a day. When she finally pulled into the tiny settlement of Glenora, eighty miles up the river, the news spread fast: A white woman was in town! Not only that—she was as tall and strong as the men who were packing supplies into the North, and she wore a broad-brimmed cow driver's hat over her auburn curls. Jim Callbreath, a local resident who became Kate's friend, said, "Any woman who could make it up the Stikine River on the ice should be treated as an equal to any packer in the territory."

Kate told Callbreath that thousands of people with "gold fever" would be arriving by boat as soon as the ice broke up. When Callbreath decided to build a hotel, Kate took the five-dollar gold piece from her secret pocket and offered Callbreath a deal: If she invested in his project, could she open a restaurant in his building? He agreed, and soon an old packing shed and warehouse were converted into the Glenora Hotel and Restaurant. Kate's restaurant became a popular meeting spot for customers who enjoyed her stews and her sourdough bread and biscuits, which rose thanks to her original fistful of starter.

At the end of April, the river ice began to groan and crack like pistol shots. Huge chunks of ice swept down the river. Before long, boats full of prospectors pulled into town. Passengers who expected a railroad were shocked to find a sleepy village of less than a hundred people, with no transportation further north. Houses and tents sprang up overnight. Callbreath went away for two weeks and, when he returned, he found someone had added onto his store (without his permission), an army unit was camped

*Kate Ryan driving her team of sled dogs, the most convenient way*
*to travel through the deep snows of the North*

in his potato field, and Kate had so many customers she didn't
have time to talk. The town also had a brand-new newspaper,
which boasted that Glenora was "the town that was built in a day."

Kate spent most of the next year in Glenora, living in her
tent. As winter cut off supplies of fresh food, she hired young
boys to catch fish and learned to cook with dried eggs, potatoes,
and onions. The restaurant was wildly successful. When spring
came, Kate could call herself a true "sourdough," the label
given to an outsider who had survived a northern winter. She

had also saved up plenty of gold without ever going into the diggings. But Kate was restless. When she heard rumors about even bigger strikes in the Klondike, she sold her restaurant and headed north again.

Kate rode out of town alone, leading a string of pack horses. She wore a short, split skirt, which allowed her to ride astride. Traveling through swamps thick with mosquitoes and heavy forests where she could hardly find the trail, Kate finally reached Teslin Lake. There, she planned to catch a boat to Dawson.

But a thin skim of ice already covered the lake. There were no boats in sight and it was too late to go back. Kate didn't have enough supplies to start another restaurant. Fortunately, Kate's friend Inspector Primrose heard she was in the area. The Mounties at his new camp needed a nurse. Primrose remembered that Kate had once worked in a hospital and sent her a message, asking her to come for the winter.

Although she never had any formal training as a nurse, Kate had cared for a woman in Seattle who was dying of tuberculosis before she worked at the Vancouver hospital. She accepted the inspector's offer right away, covering the sixty miles in five days. She had to cross a mountain pass in temperatures that started at minus 40 degrees and fell to minus 60 degrees.

Kate arrived safely and was soon living in her tent again. All winter, she took care of sick Mounties and did their washing, one of the worst jobs in the North. She melted snow for wash water, scrubbed the dirty clothes on a washboard, then wrung them out by hand and dried them near the stove. The Mounties were so happy to have clean shirts that they paid high prices for her labor.

The winter was incredibly difficult. The isolated settlement ran low on food. With no fresh fruit or vegetables, many people suffered from scurvy. Others developed frostbite. At Christmas, Kate added her tiny supply of six potatoes—sent by her family in New Brunswick—to make the meager dinner more festive. On the coldest nights, her loyal Mountie friends took turns loading her stove, to make sure her fire never went out.

Kate was relieved when spring came and she could walk along the rough trail to the town of Whitehorse. As soon as she arrived, she set up her tent, poked her stovepipe through the roof, and was in business again. This time, at a friend's suggestion, she posted a sign outside that read "Klondike Kate's Café." The name stuck, and she was soon known to all as "Klondike Kate."

Kate took out a free miner's license, which allowed her to pan for gold herself. She also loaned miners money to help them get started with their claims. In northern Canada and Alaska, the ground stays frozen all year, so prospectors needed extra cash to support themselves through the winter months while they built fires to melt the permafrost, then dug out the "paydirt." In the spring, they washed out the gold and Kate got her money back— along with a share of their earnings. She also invested in copper mines, continued to take in washing, and sometimes helped people who were sick, although she never charged for her nursing services.

After six months, Kate had earned enough money to build her own cabin. For the first time since she'd left Vancouver, she had walls, a floor, and curtains over the windows. At the same time, she moved her restaurant into a hotel. No more cooking or sleeping in a tent!

As the town grew, bars, dance halls, and gambling dens sprang up to entertain the prospectors. The drinking and gambling brought crime—and arrests. Usually, men got in trouble, but occasionally, the Northwest Mounted Police took a woman into custody. They wished they had a policewoman on the force to deal with female prisoners. When the Canadian Parliament passed a law allowing the Mounties to hire women, the Yukon detachment asked Kate Ryan to be their first "Woman Special."

Kate knew nothing about being a police officer. But then, she'd mushed a team of dogs up a river, opened restaurants, panned for gold, and performed minor surgery—all without much training. She became a Woman Special in February, 1900, exactly two years after she'd left Vancouver.

At first, Kate worked at the jail as only a part-time matron. But the Mounties soon needed her for another job. Sometimes prospectors concealed gold in their clothes when they went home, to avoid the Canadian tax. The Mounties made Kate their gold inspector and put her in charge of searching the women. She made her own uniform—a long, gray dress with armbands—and the local head of the police declared that Kate was "warm-hearted, affable, and efficient, the very woman for the job."

Kate and a male constable rode the early train to Skaguay, searching passengers and their luggage as it rumbled along. One morning, a haughty woman refused to answer Kate's questions. Kate threatened to search her, and the woman cried, "I am the wife of Major General Brompton of the United States Army!"

Kate pulled herself up to her full six feet. "And *I* am an officer of the British Crown," she announced, and took the woman into a private cabin. Sure enough, the woman had large gold nuggets hidden in her hair.

When Kate returned to Whitehorse, the stationmaster had already heard the news over the telegraph. "Morning, 'Sergeant'

*"Sergeant Kate" at the railroad station with Inspector Synder of
the Royal Canadian Mounted Police. Kate wears the uniform
she made herself.*

Kate," he said, teasing her. "Klondike Kate," the first female gold
inspector, had earned herself a second nickname.

Kate stayed on in Whitehorse for many years. Like many
women who left a more civilized life to follow the "call of the
wild," Kate never sought fame—yet she was celebrated all over
the North for her courage and her great heart. Her great-niece
described Kate as "very straitlaced," yet generous to the rough
miners who lived around her. According to one prospector, "Kate
was known everywhere as the miner's friend. Whenever she heard

*Kate at age fifty-nine, dressed for the Yukon Sourdough convention
held in Vancouver in 1928 to celebrate the original Klondike
pioneers. Kate sat at the head table with her friend, the poet
Robert W. Service. Kate's friends claimed that her stories about
the region inspired some of Service's most famous poems.*

that some poor devil was lying sick and alone on the trail she'd get to him. . . . I've known her in the wintertime to mush in with a dog team for a hundred miles and bring a sick fellow out."

In spite of all the hardships she faced, Kate always preferred life in the wilderness. She could never be happy in cities or towns. "I love the North," she said. "It is a glorious country, and has a wonderful future." Like other unsung western heroines, Kate Ryan left her own permanent mark on the frontier.

The Legacies of
Eight Pioneer Women

LOTTA CRABTREE retired from the stage after a clumsy actor dropped her and broke her back. Still, nothing could stop Lotta's irrepressible spirit. She took up painting and ran a stable of race-horses with her brother Jack. During World War One, she became involved in the suffrage movement, believing that women would stop the war if they could vote. Always a rebel, she bought a car which she nicknamed "Red Rose" and drove her-self everywhere at a time when "respectable" women didn't drive alone.

All her life, Lotta gave money away to groups that helped vet-erans, ailing actors, and homeless children. A vegetarian who loved animals, she helped organizations that cared for injured animals and built city water fountains for horses and dogs, including two which still stand in San Francisco and Boston. The second richest woman in Boston when she died in 1924 at age 76, she left four million dollars to charity.

SUSAN SHELBY MAGOFFIN didn't continue her diary after she left Mexico, so we don't know much about the last years of her life. She and Samuel moved to Missouri, where Susan lost another baby. She finally had two daughters who survived, but Susan herself died soon after the birth of her last child. She was only twenty-eight years old.

It's not clear whether Susan hoped to publish her journal, although her neat, careful handwriting suggests that she intended to share the diary with friends and family. The thick calfskin book was unknown to most Americans until 1926, when the Missouri Historical Society published the first edition, dedicated to "Jane Taylor, the Gentle Daughter of Susan Shelby Magoffin." The diary has been reprinted many times since then and remains a unique record of our past. Historians still turn to Susan's vivid entries to help them understand a way of life that has disappeared forever.

BIDDY MASON lay in an unmarked grave for almost a hundred years after her death, and Los Angeles seemed to have forgotten one of its most important citizens. Then, in 1988, the First African Methodist Episcopal Church, which Biddy had helped to found, honored her memory by unveiling a new tombstone. The church's gospel choir sang at the ceremony.

The next year, Los Angeles constructed a new parking garage and shopping plaza on the site of Biddy's original homestead and installed an eighty-one-foot wall of black concrete highlighting Biddy's achievements. Nearby, the artist Betye Saar created an intricate sculpture that includes a picket fence like the one around Biddy's home and artifacts from her life. Both memorials are located in the heart of a busy neighborhood. Robert Chattel, an architect who helped with the project, reports that "they have been treated with great reverence for ten years."

When the art was installed, Mayor Tom Bradley declared November 16, 1989, "Biddy Mason Day" and the *Los Angeles*

*Times* headline announced, "Early Black Heroine of L.A. Finally Receives Her Due."

All her life, BETHENIA OWENS-ADAIR continued to work hard for causes she believed in. She was especially concerned with the health of infants and mothers and equal rights for women. Her autobiography, which she published after she retired from medicine, is full of the letters she wrote to legislators, newspaper editors, and magazines about health and women's rights. She lived long enough to cast her ballot in the first national election open to women and to see as many as seven thousand women doctors practicing medicine. Bethenia died of heart disease in 1926 and was buried in Astoria, near the spot where she and her parents had first arrived in Oregon.

SUSAN LaFLESCHE PICOTTE devoted her whole life to improving the welfare of the Omaha people. Her husband, Henry, died young, and Susan raised her sons on her own while treating patients and working hard on projects—such as preventing the spread of alcoholism—which would improve the health of her tribe.

Sadly, Susan died of a brain disease when she was only fifty years old. She probably had mastoiditis, which can now be treated with antibiotics. After her death, the residents of Walthill renamed their hospital the Susan LaFlesche Picotte Hospital. The town still celebrates her life each September, when the community gathers for "Picotte Days," a festival which includes speakers, a powwow, Omaha games, and traditional foods.

KATE RYAN was successful as a cook, a miner, and a policewoman, but she missed having a family. When her brother's wife died, Kate took in her four nephews and raised them as her own children. After Leo, her favorite, drowned in a shipwreck, Kate left Whitehorse in despair, but she couldn't stay away from the wilderness. She took on the job of mining commissioner in Stewart, British Columbia. Once more, she began a new and challenging career, surrounded by the rugged landscape that had always inspired her.

Kate Ryan lost much of her wealth in the stock market crash of 1929. When she died in 1932 at the age of sixty-two, the *Stewart News* reported that "Miss Ryan was accorded the honor of an escort of the Royal Canadian Mounted Police" at her funeral. Kate spent her final years in poverty, but she was remembered, according to the paper, for a "great and charitable spirit that endeared her to thousands." She was buried in an unmarked grave, near the mountains she loved so well.

MARY TAPE and Joseph had a long and happy life together. The couple celebrated their fiftieth wedding anniversary in an Oakland hotel ballroom in November of 1925. Mary died three years later, and Joseph died soon afterward.

Mary left a lasting legacy behind. In 1995, more than a century after her photographs appeared in San Francisco's newspapers, her artwork was featured in an exhibit of Asian American artists called "With New Eyes." Thousands of people, including her great-grandchildren, visited the show at San Francisco State University and admired Mary's paintings and hand-painted china, lovingly preserved by her descendants.

The San Francisco school system remained segregated, with Chinese attending separate public schools, until well into the twentieth century. Many other Chinese families followed the Tapes' example, taking the city and the state to court, before Chinese students received equal treatment in the schools.

At the end of her life, BRIGHT EYES, or SUSETTE LA-

FLESCHE TIBBLES, seemed lost and confused, and was sometimes found wandering on the open prairie she had loved as a
child. She lapsed into a long illness and was tended by Tibbles
and her sister Susan, the reservation doctor. Bright Eyes was only
forty-eight when she died.

The dispute that began when Joseph LaFlesche first built his
"Village of the Make-Believe White Men" continued long after
Bright Eyes's death. Recently, tribal elders sought to heal the rift
by arranging for the return of their sacred objects from the
Peabody Museum in Cambridge, Massachusetts. In 1990, the
sacred pole known as "The Venerable Man" returned home to
Nebraska and was given to Doran Morris, a direct descendant of
Yellow Smoke, who had been the last keeper of the pole. The
seven-foot-long pole has a scalp on top, to symbolize a head, and
a wooden base like a foot. In a solemn ceremony, the Omaha
elders propped the pole at its traditional 45-degree angle, blessed
it, and welcomed it back to the tribe. Many Omahas had tears in
their eyes as they lined up to touch the pole. The ceremony
would have pleased Bright Eyes, who never forgot the important
traditions which shaped her early years.

# Acknowledgments

I AM GRATEFUL TO THE following librarians and archivists for their special help in tracking down photographs, prints, and other research material: Irene Poon Anderson, Art Department, San Francisco State University; David Burgevin, National Anthropological Archives, Smithsonian Institution; Simon Elliot, Special Collections, University of California at Los Angeles; Annette Fern, Harvard Theatre Collection, Harvard University; Susan Haas, Society of California Pioneers; Deanna Held, University of Colorado at Boulder; Michael Hironymous, Nettie Lee Benson Latin American Collection, University of Texas at Austin; Ellen Thomasson, Missouri Historical Society Library; Chad Wall, Nebraska Historical Society; Elizabeth Winroth, Oregon Historical Society. Thanks as well to the librarians at the Boston Athenaeum, the American Antiquarian Society in Worcester, Massachusetts, and the Harvard University libraries for assistance with research questions.

The following individuals were most generous in sharing their knowledge and expertise about some of the women in this book: Ann Brennan, author of *The Real Klondike Kate: The Story of Katherine Ryan*; Paul Burke, an adopted member of the Omaha

tribe; Robert Chattel, AIA, an architect and historic preservation-
ist involved in the Biddy Mason memorials in Los Angeles; Dr.
William Horgan, a Native American singer and adopted member
of the Ottowa tribe; William Loren Katz, historian and author of
many books on African Americans in the West; and Professor Judy
Yung, author of *Unbound Feet: A Social History of Chinese
Women in San Francisco.* My deepest thanks to Ken Lum, great-
grandson of Mary Tape, and to Katherine Ryan McKernan, the
great-niece of Kate Ryan, for their time and patience with my
questions about their ancestors, and for their willingness to share
pictures from their family photo albums.

Finally, thanks to my agent, Gail Hochman, and my editor,
John Keller, for their commitment to the project, and to the following friends, colleagues, and family members who provided
suggestions on the manuscript or helped in my quest for primary
source material: Eileen Christelow, Janet Coleman, Dayton Dun-
can, Julia Elsas, Susan Goodman, Robie Harris, Karen Hesse,
Will and Jean Hobbs, Forrest Holzapfel, Lisa Jahn-Clough,
Richard Ketchum, Bob MacLean, Justyn Moulds, Neil Senior,
Sarah Stone, John Straus, and Katherine Turner.

# Illustration Credits

*The pictures and photographs in this book are from the following collections, and are used with their permission:*

## COVER

Top-half scene: Photo by Ben Wittick, courtesy, Museum of New Mexico, Neg. No. 3083

Map illustration: Ethan K. Murrow

Susan Magoffin: Courtesy, Missouri Historical Society, St. Louis

Lotta Crabtree: Courtesy, Harvard Theatre Collection, Houghton Library, Fredric Woodbridge Wilson, Curator

Biddy Mason: Courtesy, William Loren Katz Collection, from *Black Women of the Old West* (Antheneum)

Bethenia Owens-Adair: G.D. Morse photo, courtesy, Oregon Historical Society #OrHi 3

Susette LaFlesche Tibbles: Courtesy, Nebraska State Historical Society

Susan LaFlesche Picotte: Courtesy, National Anthropological Archives, Smithsonian Institution

Mary McGladery Tape: Courtesy, Ken Lum

Katherine Ryan: Courtesy, Katherine Ryan McKernan

## INTRODUCTION

p. 5: photo by Ben Wittick, courtesy, Museum of New Mexico, Neg. No. 3083

### CHAPTER 1: SUSAN MAGOFFIN

p. 9: Courtesy, Missouri Historical Society, St. Louis

p. 10: Courtesy, Missouri Historical Society, St. Louis

p. 13: Map, courtesy, Yale University Press

p. 17: "Stuck Fast," drawing by G.H. Baker, by G.D. Morse, courtesy, Oregon Historical Society #OrHi 39601

p. 21: Carl Nebel, artist, "The Battle of Buena Vista," courtesy, Nettie Lee Benson Latin American Collection, General Libraries, University of Texas at Austin

p. 23: Daguerreotype by Emil Jacobs, courtesy, Chicago Historical Society

### CHAPTER 2: LOTTA CRABTREE

p. 26: J.D. Borthwick illustration, courtesy, Boston Athenaeum

p. 29: Courtesy, Harvard Theatre Collection, the Houghton Library, Fredric Woodbridge Wilson, Curator

p. 34: Courtesy, Harvard Theatre Collection, the Houghton Library, Fredric Woodbridge Wilson, Curator

p. 37: Courtesy, Harvard Theatre Collection, the Houghton Library, Fredric Woodbridge Wilson, Curator

### CHAPTER 3: BIDDY MASON

p. 42: Courtesy, William Loren Katz Collection. From *Black Women of the Old West* (Atheneum)

p. 46: Department of Special Collections, Charles E. Young Research Library, UCLA

p. 49: Department of Special Collections, Charles E. Young Research Library, UCLA

p. 50: Photograph by Robert Jay Chattel, courtesy, Robert Jay Chattel, AIA

## CHAPTER 4: BETHENIA OWENS-ADAIR

pp. 54–55: Frank H. Schwarz mural, Oregon State Capitol Building, courtesy, Oregon Historical Society #OrHi 529

p. 59: Schoolhouse, Roseburg, Oregon, 1859, courtesy, Oregon Historical Society #OrHi 100063

p. 61: G.D. Morse photograph, courtesy, Oregon Historical Society #OrHi 3

p. 65: Courtesy, Oregon Historical Society OrHi 38361

## CHAPTER 5: BRIGHT EYES: SUSETTE LaFLESCHE TIBBLES

p. 70: Courtesy, National Anthropological Archives, Smithsonian Institution

p. 73: Drawing by Susette LaFlesche Tibbles, courtesy, American Antiquarian Society

pp. 79: Courtesy, Nebraska State Historical Society

pp. 81: Courtesy, Nebraska State Historical Society

pp. 82: Courtesy, Nebraska State Historical Society

## CHAPTER 6: SUSAN LaFLESCHE PICOTTE

p. 85: Courtesy, Nebraska State Historical Society

p. 89: Courtesy, National Anthropological Archives, Smithsonian Institution

p. 93: Courtesy, Nebraska State Historical Society

p. 95: Courtesy, Nebraska State Historical Society

## CHAPTER 7: MARY TAPE

p. 99: Arnold Genthe photograph, "Yoo-Hong Low Restaurant," courtesy, Library of Congress, LC-USZ 62-54612

p. 101: Photograph by L. J. Stellman, courtesy, The Society of California Pioneers

p. 105: Photograph, courtesy, Ken Lum

p. 106: Photograph, courtesy Ken Lum

p. 108: Oil painting by Mary Tape, photograph courtesy, Ken Lum

## CHAPTER 8: KLONDIKE KATE